FAREWELL TRANSMISSION

(NOTES FROM HIDDEN SPACES)

WILL McGRATH

DZANC
BOOKS

2580 Craig Rd.
Ann Arbor, MI 48103
www.dzancbooks.org

Library of Congress Cataloging-in-Publication Data Available Upon Request

First Edition: August 2022
ISBN: 9781950539505
Cover design and illustrations by J. Zachary Keenan
Interior design by Michelle Dotter

Some names have been changed, to protect the innocent and the guilty.

Printed in the United States of America

10   9   8   7   6   5   4   3   2   1

SUCH AS:

OVERTURE

Bird & Spade   9

INVISIBILITIES

The Kings of Simcoe County   15

Huron River Drive   27

A Noose in Hentiesbaai   51

Hallucination (Donut Shop)   67

Keyhole to Sana'a   73

Death of the Virgin   89

Hallucination (Active Shooter)   101

EXCAVATIONS

Peanut's Odyssey   109

Ballad of the Curtain Jerker   133

The Open Pits   153

Steel Tracks   161

Hallucination (Hotel Room)   181

Garden of the Goatherd   179

Farewell Transmission   193

CODA

Hallucination (San Sebastian)   205

The story is not all mine, nor told by me alone.
Indeed I am not sure whose story it is; you can judge better.

—Ursula K. Le Guin

There is another world, but it is in this one.

—Paul Éluard

The story is not all mine, nor told by me alone.
Indeed I am not sure whose story it is; you can judge better.

—Ursula K. Le Guin

There is another world, but it is in this one.

—Paul Éluard

OVERTURE

BIRD & SPADE

THEN WE CAME DOWN OFF THE MOUNTAIN, the air electric in our lungs. Sam wanted to get home before darkness fell, was afraid of the devil dogs, Eve too, and who could blame them. We'd seen those dogs before in the full dark—their eyes glowing like little dimes—as they slunk between the thatch-roofed rondavels of the village and slipped down toward the river. This was when we lived in Lesotho, that tiny verdant gem set into the bezel of southern Africa's highlands. Sam was five then, Eve three, and the devil dogs had colonized perhaps an outsized stretch of their mental landscape. But that climb in the late afternoon never failed to thrill: we made the ascent daily and sat in the wind with all of Mokhotlong camptown spread below us. From an outcropping we watched hawks glide in figure eights, infinite loops, surfing invisible currents while they hunted. When the sun sat atop the rim of mountains, the brilliant falling light woke up the metal roofs of the town below, a silver mosaic set into the valley floor.

We found the bird near the doorstep to our room. It had flown into a window, tricked by that same light, and lay on its back terminally stunned. *Oh,* said Eve, when she saw the poor ruined creature. *Oh,* said Sam, as he watched the frantic pumping of its breath. I brought them inside and found a cartoon. They asked if I was going to help the bird and I said yes.

I drew a curtain across the window and closed the door. When I stepped outside, I saw the bird had managed to right itself and was gravely attempting to scrape off toward the road. It could not fly. I knew once night fell the devil dogs would take great brainless pleasure in eating it alive, so I went looking for Ntate Thumisang's spade.

The bird had made little progress by the time I returned, but two of its companions had come to protect it. They hopped about, worrying, lit off as I neared, then roosted on a downspout out of reach. They chirped furiously at me, darting toward and then away, venturing as close as they dared. I stood over the broken creature and it stilled in my shadow. For a moment I watched its delicate chest heaving—it was a sparrow, perhaps, or a wren, decorated around the throat with ruffed white. I thought of Sam and Eve inside the room.

Dusk was oozing down the mountainside, congealing in clefts and crevices, and the air had gone cold. I could hear the wilderness listening, as William Stafford once wrote, and so I floated the flat face of the spade over the wounded animal, inhaled and exhaled and brought the spade down as hard as I could then did it again before I could decide whether a second blow was necessary. Electricity sang in my forearms, traveled aching to my elbows, and dispersed. Two flat metal *pongs* echoed off the mountains. The bird was dead instantly, the lights cut. I scooped it onto the spade and headed toward the road, where the devil dogs would have it after all. Its two companions swooped and scouted for the remainder of the evening, singing out, searching, and then I didn't see them again.

I won't pretend to know what happens when we die. That bird became electricity and sound, passed through me on its way elsewhere.

But I do know they'll ask before I'm ready—perhaps I'll be sweeping under the dinner table, cleaning bits of chicken the baby shredded, and Eve will say, *Daddy, what happens after we're dead?*

Maybe we have souls that become electricity, or maybe the lights go out forever, or maybe our molecules sink into the earth and rearrange, find a new form, a different kind of eternal return. Maybe I won't say any of that, I don't know.

And maybe the question of *after* isn't the question at all.

After I returned from the road and after I returned the spade to Ntate Thumisang's shed, I slipped back into our room. Inside, a cartoon mouse was bashing a cat over the head with a frying pan, again and again, and Sam and Eve were dying, they were utterly beside themselves. Sam had his arm around Eve's shoulders. I stood in the doorway and watched.

INVISIBILITIES

THE KINGS OF SIMCOE COUNTY

I'M TWO HOURS NORTH OF TORONTO in a borrowed bug-eyed Mercedes, rolling hard on Tim Hortons and intent on dodging the fuzz. I've come here with an ill-bred band of hooligans, upstarts, blowhards, and minor louts—one of whom I'm bound to by the treaties of holy matrimony, the others by various blood oaths and pacts of mutual degeneracy. We have come to the Great White North in search of the Deep Down South. We have come to see the Kings. Up here the roads are sunbaked gray, voluptuous and empty in a way that obligates fast driving. We blur through rural intersections and skim alongside golden shag. The Ontario farmland unfurls warmly around us. We pass the steady moral ranch houses of Simcoe County, their front lawns decorated with Muskoka chairs and wooden moose statuary. Here in the side yard a gardener has populated her strawberry patch with tiny stone and crystal fairy figurines, deep in the vegetation—a secret joke, a secret hope.

"Norm!" the Karate Elvises are screaming. "Do your thing, Norm!"

Norm is perspiring and his mascara has started to run. The crowd in the bar has settled into a low anticipatory thrum as Norm centers himself between songs, but when they catch the opening strains of the gospel classic "Stand by Me," the room emits a shriek—men, women, most of them grandparents—everyone shrieks instinctively, it is bat sound. The crowd is lathered, but Norm is calm, Norm is in total control. In a certain slant of light he looks downright beatific.

Then his kid comes out on stage. Norm's kid can't be more than six.

"Wait for it," the Karate Elvises are telling me, shaking me by the arm.

I wait for it.

A question:

Why does one go to an Elvis Presley impersonator festival in the county of Simcoe, in the province of Ontario, in the country of Canada, on the planet of Earth?

That question benefits from a slight rephrasing: In a rustic town in Ontario there exists the world's largest Elvis fest, a multiday celebration involving parades of classic cars, carnival rides, Elvis flicks under the stars, hundreds of live performances, and a battle royale to determine the greatest Elvis impersonator on the planet. The rephrased question is: What kind of philistine doesn't go?

We're roosting in an empty dive bar off the main drag of this small town, waiting for the day's first Elvis. My compatriots and I have been analyzing the two primary species of performer here at the festival. There are the glory hounds vying for the crown—men who shimmy-shake in velvet-seated theaters and bellow from stages that block intersections—and then there are the anonymous scrappers, the small-time wig jockeys just hoping to get their drinks comped. If a choice must be made, the choice is clear: my sympathies will forever lie with the no-names who drop joybombs in dingy beer halls.

Outside the rain starts coming down apocalyptically, the blue Ontario sky blanketed gray. A crush of wet Elvis heads packs the bar. Perched comfortably on our stools, we preen, feeling wise in our decision to shun the main stages. We stretch our legs in contentment, we grow drunk on our perspicacity and our tequila shooters. The rain has not ruined the festival, just concentrated things along the periphery, which—journalistically speaking—is the only place to be.

The place is getting rowdy, people soaked and jostling and starting to drink. Now the first ETA of the afternoon takes the stage, steps onto a low carpeted riser. This ETA—that's Elvis Tribute Artist, no impersonators here, only homage—he looks nervous, a very un-Elvis state of mind. This man is in his fifties and he is fastidiously smoothing back the sides of his jet-black pompadour. Then the cornball karaoke backing track starts up and Elvis swan dives into "Hound Dog," a theoretically invigorating opener that isn't working at all. It's a long drop to the waves below. His vocals are too low—first act of the day, sound guy hasn't dialed in yet—and the backing track is overwhelming. Elvis is rigid and hesitant, rooted as he sings, and he knows it's wrong and we know it's wrong and things are quickly going sideways. He takes a step off the riser, wants to engage the crowd, but the mic whines and he retreats, pinned onstage.

I feel uncomfortable because Elvis is a truly nice dude. When he is not Elvis, he is a steel salesman out of Michigan—*Slinging steel!* I say to him as we chat pre-show, and he looks at me cockeyed, this nomenclature apparently not in wide circulation outside my brain. Elvis tells me his name is Fab and I choose to take him at his word. His work-related travels often bring him through Chicago, where I grew up, and Fab and I talk Chicago, we talk Gary, Indiana, we talk Michigan, we are simpatico. So it pains me to see him up there, not dying exactly, but certainly not living.

Then—mid-song, mid-lyric—Fab sees me in the crowd, winks and shoots his finger guns at me, says, "Hey there, Chicago."

That's all it takes, a familiar face. Fab is cranked up now, posing and vamping, mimicking those iconic Elvis stances, hip-sprung, lunging and beckoning. He does a wizardly move, some spell-conjuring gesture, and the crowd digs it—this is a friendly room after all, no one's looking for a train wreck. Fab sashays, bobs his head like a prizefighter.

Now that he's rolling I take a moment to appreciate his outfit. Fab is doing the 1970s Vegas Elvis thing, sporting a white polyester jumpsuit, thoroughly rhinestoned and hugging thickly to his midsection. His plunging neckline introduces lustrous tufts of salt and pepper. It is Fab's edge-game that sets him apart, though: everything is tasseled and fringed and braided, fringed tassels and tasseled braids, the whole getup in liquid motion around him. He sports a belt of woven green, its long plaits hula dancing near his knees. The cumulative effect is that of blurred borders.

Fab has been doing this for nine years now. He'd sung in country bands all his life, a passive Elvis fan but no aficionado, the kind of guy who toe taps to "Jailhouse Rock" but doesn't know the deep cuts. Then one year, when he'd been feeling restless, in a down period between bands, a relative dragged him to an Elvis fest and something connected. He went out directly, bought the costume, dyed his hair. Now he hits five or six festivals a year. The wife even comes sometimes. "When it's someplace nice," he tells me. "She came to the one in Myrtle Beach."

When his set is done, I go to buy Fab a drink but I have to wait— some other stranger has beaten me to it. He bearhugs me when I reach him and thanks me for sticking around, but other fans want a piece of his time. Fab is moving briskly now, doling out high fives, receiving back slaps, radiant and sweaty, transported.

The storm clouds have blown off for a moment so we take to the streets, pillaging the food stands of Simcoe County: hot dogs, pulled pork, lemonade, ice cream, fried dough in various contortions. There is region-specific fare as well, and the culinary geniuses among us opt for a Canadian three-piece: peameal bacon sandwich up front, poutine on support, beavertail chaser—forthwith to the cardiac ward.

We return to the bar just in time to catch Elvis come bolting onto the low carpeted riser, fist-pumping to the gameshowy opening brass of "See See Rider." Elvis is a stocky First Nations man with a thick watermelon gut, thick gold sunglasses, thick black pomp. Very quickly he is sweating hard, aiming for verisimilitude that would make the King proud. His pipes are rich baritone and listening to him is an experience not unlike being rubbed in butter.

The room is humid, dense with people, and Elvis stalks through the crowd draping gossamer scarves across the shoulders of swooning women. Everyone is slicked with rain or sweat or tears or all three. As he works the crowd, Elvis's wife is discreetly restocking him with scarves. She's a pro: she's got a duffle filled with scarves slung over her shoulder, yet she remains out of the spotlight as she feeds him, for no swooner wants the performance marred by the reality of a happily married Elvis.

Elvis mops his face with each new scarf before giving it away. He is killing us with "In the Ghetto," his finale, we are bawling like babies out here, he can do with us as he pleases.

[mop]
on a cold and gray Chicago mornin'
a poor little baby child is born
[mop]
in the ghetto
[mop]

And like that Elvis is done. While we in the crowd are basking in post-coital glow, his attendants have hustled him out the door. I run into the street, push through the crowds, I need to talk with him, touch his hand, but it is too late—Elvis has left the building.

A scrum of groupies comes down the street, women in their sixties wearing autographed white T-shirts, black Sharpie markers in hand, begging signatures from the performers. Now they stop to pose for pictures with Elvis, who is in his mid-twenties and has Down syndrome. He's dressed in all black: black pants, black blazer, black T-shirt, black hair gelled into a tower. Elvis is laughing as the groupies offer their markers to him. Over on the sidewalk, Elvis's mother and two of his aunts are beaming as they watch the scene unfold.

By the time the Karate Elvises swagger into the bar it feels inevitable, feels like they've come looking for us. They appear to have a bit of drink in them already.

"We're stunt Elvises!" one of the three yells at me. "We do karate kicks and ride our dirt bikes over cliffs!"

They are dressed in familiar motif—the white rhinestoned jumpsuits, the chunky gold sunglasses—but two of them have nunchaku tucked beneath knotted yellow belts that have perhaps been stolen from a child's martial arts class.

"Cool nunchucks," I say, and so they begin whirling their nunchaku in the air, flipping them under their arms and around their backs, and it feels like a victory when no one is injured in any significant way. The Karate Elvises are pushing thirty, potbellied and scruffy. One has a full beard. Another is sporting a bushy Fu Manchu mustache and has his head Bic'd up the sides, his long hair greased straight back. All three are wearing plastic leis and plastic sheriff's badges. At their request we join them in shots of Jägermeister, which feels unseemly and like the only appropriate outcome of our encounter.

They do this often, the Karate Elvises tell me, hit up the various festivals, but they never perform. They're just here to party and see some Elvises they know from the scene. One Karate Elvis is a middle school teacher, another works for a company that makes industrial plastic molds. I briefly consider connecting him with Fab, the steel salesman, but I don't know if the steel crowd and the plastics crowd run together.

When I ask them how they first got involved with Elvis fest, this happens:

Fu Manchu takes a step back from the group, turns his back, spreads his wings. He stands before us with a heavy satin cape that spans arm to arm, falls past his waistline in a perfect semicircle. While Fu Manchu presents his cape, Bearded Elvis goes into a low boxer's crouch beside the cape, fists up, rings sparkling. This is their answer to my question.

After a period of silence, Bearded Elvis yells with exasperation: "It's his wife's wedding dress!"

"My fucking *EX*-wife, man," Fu Manchu corrects over his shoulder, still spread wide.

I reach out and touch it; the fabric is creamy and expensive, a dream on the fingertips. It is indeed part of a wedding dress, hacked off from the rest of the gown, now heavily bejeweled, little constellations of plastic gemstones glued everywhere. It has been professionally re-hemmed.

Fu Manchu's wife was cheating on him, he tells me, and when they split up he fell into a bad hard time. The other Karate Elvises—pre-Elvises at the time—came by one day to help pack up the house. They found the wedding dress hanging in an empty closet. *Toss that thing!* Fu Manchu said, but Bearded Elvis stayed his hand. The three of them stood looking at it, awaiting inspiration.

Looks like something Liberace woulda worn.

Yeah, or fucking Elvis.

This is how healing begins.

Someone has ordered more Jägermeister, heaping sin upon sin, and a new Elvis is crooning softly from the riser. A team of tween boys in soccer uniforms has infiltrated the bar somehow, selling raffle tickets for a local fundraiser. One boy's mom stands watching from the wall—a canny operator separating a roomful of drunks from their money—but just out of her view the Karate Elvises are showing the goalie and midfielder how to play touchscreen bar games.

"If you win, you get to see naked chicks," they tell the boys.

Now the Karate Elvises are leading us through the streets of this small town, strolling diagonally across intersections, holding up traffic. Things are getting lawless. It is dark but the masses are still afoot and the clouds have blown off for good. The Karate Elvises say we've gotta see their buddy Norm and his kid.

As we wander the town, our entourage begins to speculate about the central mysteries of this festival, Jägermeister being a surefire lubricant for bargain-basement philosophy. *What drives someone to be-wig himself and sing karaoke to a crowd of strangers?* we wonder aloud. *And why do those strangers come to watch?*

It must begin with Elvis Aaron Presley himself, whose life hewed so closely to an Aristotelian tragic arc as to seem a parody of it: poor hick mama's boy, born in a shotgun shack in Tupelo, Mississippi, rises to fame through a fusion of singular artistic vision and cultural theft, emerges as the bestselling solo artist in the history of recorded music, before falling under the spell of Svengalis and speed freaks, a drug-addled paranoiac shut-in who will ultimately die on his bathroom floor. Yet while the arc is familiar, there is something ineffable that situates Elvis in another realm. Compare him with a proxy like Mick Jagger. Jagger has the same outsized sexuality, the swagger, the legendary pharmaceutical abuse, the international fame, the deep catalog of revered music—but there are no Mick Jagger impersonator festivals worldwide, never will be. And you can't pin it to death mystique either. Elvis was neither the first nor the last pop icon to exit in lurid circumstances—Jimi Hendrix, Janis Joplin, Marilyn Monroe, Jim Morrison, Robert Johnson, Patsy Cline, Sid Vicious, Kurt Cobain, Marvin Gaye, John Lennon, Biggie Smalls, Michael Jackson—but none of those famously departed have inspired the same zombie cult. No one claims Jimi Hendrix secretly lived out his days as a retired accountant in Boca Raton. The only American figure to even approach a similar level of death denial is Tupac Shakur.

Into the uniquely fertile soil of Elvis Aaron Presley, then, let us introduce the instinct for public hamming, the insatiable drive to perform (cf. all reality television ever, specifically the endless talent show varietals). Crosspollinate this with another human urge, the societally approved id-unburdening event—Carnival, Halloween, Saturnalia, Mardi Gras, Holi, Burning Man, St. Paddy's Day—those public release valves that allow us to play dress-up and swap genders and step into different lives. Let all the above germinate under the warm capitalist sun of the late twentieth century and soon sprouts the Elvis Fest, the Elvis Tribute Artist, the pilgrims who trek from Texas to rural Ontario to watch people in costume pantomime a ghost.

More than forty-five years out from his death, the whole enterprise has become decoupled from Elvis Presley the Human Being and is now more about Elvis Presley the Cultural Meme. The Elvis Meme accommodates an array of ages, body types, and worldviews: you can be old Elvis, young Elvis, fat Elvis, skinny Elvis, Hawaiian Elvis, rockabilly Elvis, army Elvis, jailhouse Elvis, Vegas Elvis, greaser Elvis, country Elvis, Elvis the sexual rock rebel, Elvis the spiritual gospel crooner—so many personae linked in one body that anyone can play. Performers like Kool Keith or the ETA Dwayne Turner have found ways to transcend Elvis's whiteness. And Elvis Herselvis, the famous lesbian ETA, has long spoken of the King's "queeny" side, identifying in him a femininity that goes deeper than the mascara and the pink outfits.

And maybe that's what Elvis is really about, the grand human potential to make and remake one's identity, the mutability of—

But the Karate Elvises call bullshit on us.

"It's more about getting people to buy you drinks," Bearded Elvis says.

"Yeah," says Fu Manchu. "You're doing it wrong."

The Karate Elvises have led us through the underworld, have led us finally to Norm. In this bar, Norm is crushing one monster ballad after another, the room hanging on his every gesture. But Norm doesn't do big gestures. Everything about him is calm, confident. His face is glossed with sweat and his mascara is raccooning under his eyes, casting his face with the mournful determined look of a martyr. He's in a green silk shirt and green pants, a thin white belt delineating the two. His voice eases from the higher angelic registers into sweet low dissolution, quavering briefly, the delicate vibrato of a reed instrument—then he pulls back, perfect control, just working us.

The crowd howls in the spaces between phrases, then falls into reverential silence. Norm is keeping everyone in check with subtle motions of his hand, first pointing loosely upward with extended index finger, then pressing gently down toward the earth, as if calming a spooked animal. Up goes the finger, down goes the palm. It takes me a moment to recognize it: he's doing Plato and Aristotle from the sixteenth-century Vatican fresco *The School of Athens*—and really, if you're going to crib some material, Raffaello Motherfucking Sanzio is not a bad place to start.

Norm finishes "Stand by Me" and goes immediately into a mid-tempo triumphal rendition of "How Great Thou Art," the song that won Elvis a Grammy in 1975 when he was deep into pharmaceutical dependency and heading toward the final spiral. *I see the stars, I hear the rolling thunder.* The crowd waves their hands side to side, praising.

The Karate Elvises tell me they first partied with Norm and his dad—another well-known ETA—at an Elvis fest in Windsor a few years back. They've kept in touch since. I ask if they see that often: two generations of performers, father-son duos.

This is when Norm brings out his six-year-old kid.

"Three generations," Fu Manchu says.

The kid comes out to huge roars. The crowd has been waiting, knew this moment was coming. Sweet small boy in a striped polo shirt. He looks terrified. The crowd is with him but it's hard not to read a little Roman Colosseum into this moment, hard not to notice how drunk everyone is, hard not to see how exposed the kid looks up there. His eyes are down, hands shoved as far into his pockets as they will go. Norm introduces him, says his son is going to do a number for us. The kid keeps looking up at his dad, then back down at the floor.

But there is a problem cueing up the track "Rubberneckin" (a tune from the 1969 film *Change of Habit*, in which a benevolent young doctor at an impoverished urban clinic [Elvis Aaron Presley] falls in love with a wholesome and spirited volunteer [Mary Tyler Moore] who is also secretly a nun). We're drowning in dead air, hisses of static. It feels like the kid's been standing up there for ages. To cut the tension Norm conducts a mini interview with his son, asks him to tell the crowd why he wanted to become an Elvis Tribute Artist.

The kid exhales into the mic. "Well I just saw you and Grandpa doing it," he says quietly, halting and ummm-ing. "And I wanted to do it." The kid's voice is earnest, he means it, but it sounds rehearsed, a line coached ahead of time. His eyes keep cutting over to his dad, desperate to see how he's doing, and I'm starting to feel queasy. It is impossible not to imagine my own small boy up there. And just as I am about to run up and beg the crowd to go home, please, let this poor kid be six years old—the music starts, and the transformation happens. Norm's kid is hip-snapping on the downbeats, punching on the cymbal crashes, belting. He's up on tiptoes doing the classic pelvic swivel. The kid's a born mimic. Halfway through the song the mic goes out, but Norm is there with a backup, passes it seamlessly, kid doesn't miss a beat. Now Norm is directing the crowd, gets them into a soul clap, and the kid does a little soft shoe routine during the breakdown. I reconsider the miscued backing track, the dead air, the awkward small talk, wonder if it could be part of the act. The magician who deliberately fumbles a trick before going in for the kill. But I saw the kid's eyes—some things can't be faked.

When they close out the show with a rambunctious father-son duet of "Viva Las Vegas," it feels like the roof might lift off this joint. Norm and his kid are in perfect sync. All of us in the crowd are pressed close together—middle school teachers and salesmen, grandmothers and lawyers, music junkies and bro-bonding divorcees—all us drunks and weirdos in joyous masquerade.

HURON RIVER DRIVE

1.

When I was twenty-five, I took a job working at a homeless shelter in Ann Arbor—that minor masterpiece of the Midwest—where men in business suits and hiking sandals stride briskly through the small commercial district, cheerfully dodging the shaggy inebriates of the University of Michigan. The city is cut with a river and pocketed with forest, the downtown quickly ceding to rolling woody groves, nature preserves, and train trestles that disappear through walls of tree.

My title at the shelter was Outreach Case Manager, which meant I was the case worker for the outside—for those people who used the shelter's services (ate meals, smoked on the patio, sought medical advice from the tiny clinic) but who wouldn't or couldn't come inside. My clients lived in camps in the woods, slept under train bridges, bedded down in the unlocked laundry rooms of apartment complexes. Art spent his nights in a family's unattached garage, slipped out in the predawn. Jerome staked his tent in a copse of trees at the center of an I-94 off-ramp, the cambered road coiling in around his tiny green island. Shirley wove a nest of blankets into a church's window well.

There were many reasons people wouldn't come inside. My clients (what a lovely piece of circumlocution—as if our respective secretaries had ironed out the details) were men and women who couldn't piss clean to save their lives, or who were burrowed deep into schizoid fugues. Some were fresh from lengthy prison stays and would not abide another minute of close human quarters, could not for one more second bunk up with fat Timmy Two-Shoes, whose chainsaw snoring shredded nightly sanity and undercut the possibility for belief in a just universe. For some people it was all of the above. Anyway, it was not my place to diagnose.

My position was funded by the county health department and it was my job, to a certain extent, to see that people didn't die outside. Shortly before I began working at the shelter, during a Michigan February, a man had polished off a bottle of Kamchatka in his tent, oblivious to the sudden thaw that had soaked his sleeping bag. The temperature dropped precipitously in the night and the next morning a camp buddy found the man frozen to the ground.

But that was an extreme case. My job mainly involved visiting camps hidden throughout the county—scrabbling down embankments or picking my way through underbrush—and checking in on people's general health. Did they need sunscreen or bottles of water in the summer? Socks or long johns in the winter? Could I enroll them in the county's free healthcare plan? Did they need a ride to some preventive medical appointment, ideally, or more likely to the ER if they were falling out hard? During the year and a half I worked at the shelter, I stuffed my future wife's Pontiac Sunfire with donated boots, sleeping bags, and wilderness first aid supplies. I gave innumerable rides to unshowered strangers and deconstructed the finer points of the Detroit Pistons' pick-and-roll defense with criminal sexual offenders. It was generally an enjoyable job.

A friend had told me about the opening. She was working as a case manager there and knew I had worked at another homeless shelter a few years prior, when I lived in Arizona.

"Here's the thing," she said. "Can you lift a man?"

I was silent on the phone for a moment.

"I'm looking at the job requirements. I guess you might have to pull someone out of the woods."

"Hmm," I said. "I don't know."

I got the job anyway.

I met Willie during my first week at the shelter, and by then he had already been given his death sentence. I was speed-walking through the day room—where people sat in lorazepam stupors or tapped out the Morse code of opiate withdrawal while they played euchre—when I tossed a plastic soda bottle into the trash.

All the junkies in the room, who had been busy walking circles through the linoleum, trying not to think about Casino Ken, that big dumb look on Casino Ken's face when he's holding, how at this exact moment CK was over in Ypsi and how fucking simple would it be to walk out the door and hop on the 3 bus and—

When I tossed that plastic soda bottle into the trash.

Everyone in the room looked up at me.

It bears noting that in Michigan the refund for recycling a plastic bottle or aluminum can is ten cents, which results in a particularly robust recycling scene among Ann Arbor's homeless population. It is not uncommon to see Marshy or Karen the Tweaker or Buford rattling their shopping carts through the alleys behind the frat houses early Sunday morning, raiding the weekend's debauched refuse and hauling out fifty dollars' worth of empty Natty Light cans.

I was heading for the stairwell, walking with the jaunty vigor of someone new at his job, when I realized that everyone was staring at me. Then I saw Willie sitting over by the windows, saw him beckon me with a subtle motion of his head.

I had never talked with Willie before, but I knew who he was.

Everyone at the shelter did. I had seen him out on the smoking patio laughing and commiserating with folks coming from the AA meeting. Willie was always slapping someone on the back, always shaking someone's hand—he was a man fully engaged in the rituals of greeting, of acknowledging that you were sharing space together. For this reason alone he was immensely well liked around the shelter. For people who spend their days drifting in isolation it is a disorienting and beautiful thing to have someone contradict the basic premise of your invisibility.

Willie even used that exact wording with me once—"I'm well liked around here"—but that was much later, after I knew him differently. At fifty-three, he was one of those respected oldheads whom even the gang-affiliated kids seemed to respect, although Willie carried no air of former violence about him. He was handsome, always neatly dressed, and with his thin perfect mustache he looked something like a Black Clark Gable. Women were ruthless in their flirtations with him. Willie was one of the hidden homeless, the people you pass on the street and in a momentary glance subconsciously categorize as a citizen of middle-class America. But a momentary glance wouldn't take in the way his khaki cuffs were just a bit too frayed, the knees of his pants a shade too shiny for the respectable workplace. A momentary glance wouldn't register how often his lone button-down shirt had been washed in a bathroom sink and hung overnight to dry.

I altered course and went over to where Willie was sitting. He got up slowly and, as if we were intimate friends, slung his arm around my shoulders and walked me back to the trash can.

"Where you heading in such a rush, my man?" he asked as we walked.

Then, smiling, he released me and casually dipped his arm into the trash to retrieve the plastic soda bottle.

"Pardner," he said, his voice friendly and firm, "round here we don't throw no dimes in the trash." Then Willie slapped me hard on the back—I was dismissed—and sauntered back to his seat.

I understood in that moment exactly how oblivious and arrogant I looked. Ten cents is ten cents. It doesn't take too many recovered plastic bottles to buy some rollies, even to get a taste of crack, some momentary relief from the stunning boredom of homeless life. The way Willie corrected me had been somehow discreet and public—he was speaking privately to me and also to the whole room, wanted to teach me how to behave while demonstrating that I could be taught. Even then I recognized it as an act of kindness.

At the stairwell, I glanced back. Willie was monitoring the Ann Arbor skyline, the late winter cloud cover flattening the light into an indistinct gray. I watched him slip the plastic soda bottle into his satchel.

2.

Willie dies at the end of this story, but you probably figured that already. He was alone at the end too, unless the janitor was there, tracing gentle waxen arcs through the hallway with his buffer. I suppose it's possible Nurse Dan was there. Maybe they both attended to him— the janitor and Nurse Dan. Maybe they prayed together over Willie, the buffer murmuring in the background, maybe Nurse Dan ran a final moistened swab across Willie's lips, maybe they held his hands.

3.

Willie slumps into the passenger seat of the Sunfire. Another appointment with the oncologist, another chemo treatment scheduled. "I'm going crazy, man," he says. He looks over at me. "I got to find a *job.*" Willie sighs and buckles his seatbelt. "You know what my foster father told me once? When you stop being busy, you die. That's God's truth."

Willie and I cruise through Ann Arbor, heading generally toward lunch at the shelter. Although he spends much of his time there, Willie doesn't sleep at the shelter—he is Outside—and so his casefile has fallen under my domain. For a month now I've been driving him to all manner of medical engagements—oncologists, X-rays, general care, county health insurance specialists.

"Go left here," he says. "Let's see if we can't find me something."

We head down Main Street, Willie vetting the shops and restaurants: a fancy seafood place, an art gallery, an Irish pub, a storefront filled with humanely sourced knickknacks from developing countries.

"Maybe they need a salesman," he says. "I could sell the hell out of some African drums."

But Willie doesn't ask me to stop the car, so we keep driving.

I watch Willie pace the downtown. I see him when I'm meeting with other clients, see him on the weekends when I'm out with friends. Constantly walking, head down against the winds of early spring. He walks with a tight smile on his face, but a look of chronic exhaustion has begun to harden around his eyes. The doctor had been clear: late-stage colon cancer.

"Gotta get my exercise," Willie tells me. "Always stay moving."

I think about Willie's family, a topic on which he has remained elusive, full of half-answers and subject changes. I ask around but no one knows much. *Maybe an ex-wife,* someone says, *maybe a stepdaughter?* These kinds of details are hard to come by in a homeless shelter, where personal histories are delivered heavily redacted.

In the late spring we arrive into a period of sedate bliss. Perhaps it seems strange to characterize it this way when Willie's veins are being pumped with chemicals that scrape him out, leave him shuffling through the day—but if it isn't exactly bliss, it is at least a kind of peace.

One day, instead of dropping Willie at the hospital's main circle, I ask if he wants me to come inside with him. He stares out the passenger window, off toward a reflecting pool.

"Naw, man, it's good. You'd be sitting in there bored."

"I'll just read in the waiting room."

"Naw, I mean—"

He trails off, still looking away, and we don't say anything further about it. But when I pull into the garage and park the car, we head inside together as if this has always been our routine, and from then on it is.

Inside, the receptionist and the nurses fuss over Willie—for he is beloved here too, beloved among all staffs everywhere. I don't tell the oncology people who I am and they don't ask, just leave me to my reading. Later Willie emerges from the room, ghostly, and we make our way down to the food court, since Wendy's vanilla milkshakes are the only thing he can stomach post-chemo. Their strange synthetic chemistry provides some counterbalance to whatever is coursing through his circulatory system. We don't talk about what happens inside the room. That space is sealed off.

Afterward in the Sunfire, Willie cranks the passenger seat all the way back, lies flat, and we cruise Huron River Drive. We're playing hooky, headed away from the shelter, hidden amidst high spires of pine. Willie tells me about his *Dee*-troit youth: he was a bad boy, he says, ripping and running, but it's hard to imagine him in any real state of transgression. We drive for an hour, pushing the Sunfire hard into riverine curves, listening to Stax soul singles and dwelling in the mild bliss of that late spring. But when we get to the slow-burn crescendo at the end of "I've Been Loving You Too Long"—when the key change comes and those melancholy triumphal horns kick and Otis is down on his knees begging—at that point there's no more talking to be done, so we drive in silence.

One May afternoon I drop Willie at chemo; I have other shelter responsibilities to attend to and can't come inside with him. When I return a few hours later, I find him sitting on a bench in front of the hospital. I wave from the car but he doesn't respond, so I get out and walk over.

Willie stares through me as I come. He is furious, I can see, upset I wouldn't wait with him, his face emptied of warmth. Then I realize Willie doesn't know who I am.

I say his name and his head moves, his gaze starts to dial in, but a cloudbank of confusion and momentary fear slides across his face.

Then he smiles a dopey smile, gets up slowly, says, "Hey, there you are."

4.

Even now I don't quite know how to tell this story. What true things to include and what true things to omit. The widow's house, for instance, when Willie opened for me a secret window into his life. Kerrytown was leaf-sprung and newly wet with rain that day. Other things must remain obscure, like the story of the final check he received. He wouldn't have wanted that known, and even now I feel uncertain about how I behaved, although I did what Willie asked of me.

5.

We're in Kroger looking to splash out, spend some money, every day now a victory. Willie's careening madly through the aisles in a borrowed mobility scooter, playing chicken with a glass pyramid of pickle jars, and I'm chasing after with his crutches. He's got a broken foot, the universe having conspired to shit on him all in one final go. Willie is doing a Bond-villain cackle as he buzzes customers or whatever food display appears most precarious and I'm running damage control in case the management is watching, doing a poor job concealing my amusement at his chaotic speedrun through the produce section.

Hit by a car in Ypsi is the story he gave me, smacked in the leg and spun to the ground as he stepped from between two parked cars. This was over toward Prospect where Casino Ken hangs out. Not long before, Willie had received an influx of cash, a few hundred bucks, money from a source I didn't inquire into.

Toward the back of the store Willie caroms his scooter off the side of the meat cooler and comes briefly to rest, begins a running commentary as we shop.

"Gonna get down on that pork, you know? And those links are looking good, those links looking all right."

I fill my arms with frozen animal pieces and dump them into the scooter's basket.

"You know I love a Salisbury steak!"

People are casting sidelong glances at us, which only increases the volume of Willie's litany. He starts to dial up the "country" in his diction.

"Eat me a feast to-*night!* Get them bacon bits, get them greens."

Willie has no intention of eating this food, tonight or likely ever. He'd staggered out of chemo earlier on his crutches, ashen, couldn't handle even a Wendy's milkshake, his mouth and gums aching, his stomach in freefall. He has nowhere to cook this bounty either.

We head for the checkout line, cart brimming. We swagger up

to the register with our scooter and our armful of crutches, kings of Kroger, prepared to watch the cashier scan item after item, *beep* after *beep* after *beep*—but Willie gets hit with an emergency piss and we scramble out of line. I've been with him before when this happens, "urge incontinence" the oncologist calls it, this sudden and overwhelming need to urinate post-chemo. We rush to the Kroger bathroom and get the scooter wedged halfway through the door. Now Willie's crutches are slipping on the slick bathroom tile, so I prop him up at the urinal, the door jammed open for the entire checkout area to see, and even as I'm holding him under the armpits Willie is laughing, *goddamn*, his body is shaking, *goddamn*.

We're getting snacks at a gas station. Willie's just in a walking boot now, healing gradually, the crutches gone. He's still got some money in his pocket and insists on paying, gets mad when I start to object. But as we head through the parking lot Willie can barely make it a few steps before he has to stop, folded over, hands on his knees, "examining" something on the ground.

We walk a few more steps, and he stops again, bent over and trying to regroup. I look away, become deeply engrossed in the fine print on a Bud Light ad taped to the gas station window. After a moment, Willie picks up a broken pen from the ground in front of him, completing our little piece of theater. He straightens himself slowly, exhales.

"That's a perfectly good pen," he says, tucking it into his shirt pocket. "Someone just threw it on the ground."

6.

Willie's been holed up for two days in a grungy flophouse downtown, the Ambassador, an aspirationally named establishment that operates as a crash pad for people transforming their biweekly checks into crack cocaine. I'm knocking on Room 207—he repeated it, made sure I knew where he was—but there's no response.

Down at the front desk, I explain to the manager that, I know this sounds odd, but I need to get into Willie's room. She hesitates for a moment, then hands me a key. She is aware of the nature of our relationship.

I still can't get a response from inside Room 207, so I unlock the door, say his name as I ease inside. Willie is lying on a single mattress in his briefs, the bedding tangled around his ankles as he shifts in the semi-dark. The tiny room is filled with a dank human fug. A muted TV washes the room in ghostly light.

I sit down beside the bed and say Willie's name. He turns toward me and seems to register my presence, then drifts away, then rolls again and groans.

"Like whitewashed tombstones," he says, slurring, "like whitewashed tombs."

"Okay, Willie, I hear you."

He drifts off again.

After a while I place my hand on his shoulder. "I think we need to get you to the hospital."

Now Willie is alert. "No," he says, "no, no, no." His eyes are locked on mine.

I leave my hand on his shoulder and he sleeps again, suspended in a twilit state. A framed poster of Bavaria is the room's sole decoration, appears stolen from some defunct travel agency. A small mountain village, cows on the hillside, smiling men in lederhosen and women with blond braids. I lose myself in the glow of the TV. People are kicking a ball.

Willie rolls over, present again. "Take something," he whispers to me, nodding toward the mini fridge. "Food in there, some drinks. I can't eat it." He closes his eyes. His forehead is creased and damp.

I sit vigil for an hour while Willie passes in and out of coherence. Eventually I get up to leave.

"Don't take me to the hospital," Willie says.

I look at him, curled on the mattress, and nod.

Out on the street I stare at nothing, trying to parse my responsibilities. I wonder again at who or where or what is Willie's family.

Two days ago, when I had dropped him at the Ambassador, I asked what his plan was if there were no vacancies. Where would he go?

Willie looked at me, a strange curl of confidence around his mouth. "Oh they'll find a place for me." He paused. "I'm well liked around here."

7.

The next day I get a phone call. Willie is in the hospital. The flophouse manager called an ambulance. It's hard to blame her.

When I get to his room, Willie is holding court, charming the assembled medical professionals. He looks wrung out, but he's laughing and clear-eyed, much invigorated from whatever pit he'd fallen into at the Ambassador. *My man*, he says when sees me. The staff have been expecting me and I'm welcomed into the room. We make small talk. Everyone is smiling. They say Willie had a rough go but they're going to get him shipshape, get him comfortable. We shake hands and people filter out of the room.

As soon as we're alone, Willie gets hold of my arm, pulls me close. "You gotta get me out of here."

A nurse comes into the room to fill his water and Willie is all smiles again, all *Yes, ma'am* and *Thank you kindly!*

When she leaves, he grabs my hand.

"Get me the fuck out of this place."

I spend the day in the hospital with Willie, talking to doctors, talking to the social worker, trying to make it clear that Willie wants to be discharged as soon as possible. This is a message the staff seem disinclined to hear. *We want Willie to be comfortable*, they keep telling me, always some variation on that line, which means they want to sedate Willie through his death.

In the empty room we conduct furious whisper conversations, trying to figure out how to jailbreak, but as soon as any staff are present Willie slips into his smiley *Aw shucks!* persona.

I leave for a while in the afternoon and return to find Nurse Dan at Willie's bedside. Nurse Dan is a burly man with a thick biker mustache and a buzzcut. He has a high sweet voice and gray eyes that seem patched in from another human being. He and Willie are in sympathetic, almost conspiratorial conversation.

I explain to Nurse Dan that Willie would like to be discharged as soon as possible. He nods and asks to speak privately with me.

In the hallway Nurse Dan asks how well I know Willie.

"Better than you." It's a juvenile response, but I'm edgy and grasping.

"No, what I mean is—" He breaks off, trying to find the proper phrasing. "I don't know what your relationship with Willie is. But I have a lot of experience working with people who struggle with—"

He stops again, working out an equation in his head that involves medical privacy, trying to decide what he can disclose.

"When someone in Willie's condition is admitted to the Emergency Department, it's common to run a blood toxicology screen."

"And there was cocaine present, yes. I am not scandalized by this information."

"Okay, again, this is why I asked how well you know him." Nurse Dan rubs his buzzcut. "There is a certain degree of desperation in Willie's thinking and in his wording that, to me, indicates he plans to continue using cocaine immediately upon being discharged from the hospital. Theoretically discharged."

We stand there in the hallway.

"Willie is going to die very soon," I say. "He knows that. I know that. There is no lack of clarity on that point. And Willie's only wish in the short time remaining to him is to not die in this hospital."

Nurse Dan nods.

"So why should Willie have to die on your drugs instead of his drugs?"

Nurse Dan stares at me and doesn't answer. Then he leaves the hallway and goes to Willie's bedside.

"Well," he says, "if there's any hope of you getting out of here, you're going to have to beat the psych eval first."

So we scheme, the three of us, plotting how Willie can present himself to the psych doctor as being of sound mind and clear head. But the exam keeps getting pushed back—*Maybe twenty more minutes?* we hear again and again—and soon it's late in the day and paranoia has begun to cloud my already fuzzed thinking. They're trying to wait me out, they don't want me coaching Willie. But Willie is upbeat, certain he'll convince the psych that he poses no danger to himself. Willie the charmer, confident to the end.

Eventually I have to go home. I feel exhausted and guilty, ashamed of leaving Willie alone. But Willie is unfazed.

"Get some rest," he says. "I'll be out of here tomorrow."

8.

When I return the next morning I find Willie sedated into unconsciousness, bound to his bed with leather straps, thick scarred loops around his ankles and wrists like the kind they use for executions. I don't know if they strapped him down the exact moment I left the hospital or if perhaps they waited until dark of night. Purple bruises bloom up and down his arms, bunches of lilacs. It is clear he fought them.

"What the fuck—" I say to the first nurse that comes past the door, but there is no end to that sentence, that question, there is nothing.

I sit with Willie all week. Mostly he sleeps but sometimes he passes into groggy awareness.

I pass Nurse Dan in the hallway and he looks genuinely sad to see me, wants to talk, but I keep walking.

Later in the week Willie is closer to normal. We joke about going down to the food court to get some Wendy's, about going for a drive along the river. Willie has moments of cogency but he is not the same.

We watch lots of TV.

We don't talk about what they did to him.

Some things can't be unwound.

On Friday evening I visit Willie. Some nuns are in his room, making rounds in the hospital, singing hymns with patients. They sit in a circle, holding hands with each other and with Willie, who is lying in bed. His restraints are off by this point, no longer a threat.

"Oh!" he yells when he sees me. "Come pray with us!" His eyes are crazed, desperate.

I sit with the sisters, hold hands with them, and we sing hymns I don't know. Willie sings lustily, half-yelling, smiling at me. The sisters are harmless, I suppose, but I feel only rage. We are a scene in a TV show. I can feel myself watching this tableau from the doorway, can see the back of my own head as I sing. I stay in the circle for a while as a pocket of disgust expands in my stomach, for reasons that were unclear to me then and which remain so now.

I tell Willie I have to go. It's late, it's Friday night. There are people waiting for me.

I touch his shoulder and he grabs onto my hand.

"Stay with me," he says. "You don't have to go yet."

The sisters don't look at either of us, they stare down at their laps.

I slip my hand out of his. "I'll see you tomorrow, okay?"

9.

10.

When they call me the next morning, I go to a sub-basement deep under the hospital to retrieve Willie's belongings. The clerk hands me a clear plastic garbage bag that contains his clothes, his wallet, some bits of junk I had seen in his room at the Ambassador.

I ask the clerk what will happen to Willie's body and the clerk says that if no one claims it for ten days, his body will be donated to science.

What grand phrasing—*Donated to Science!* A gift to the ages, a boon to the expansion of human knowledge.

So that's what happens to Willie.

11.

One afternoon in late July we hold a service for Willie at the shelter. It's one of those hot, still days when the sun comes driving through the leaves and liquefies the surrounding air. A lot of people show up— Willie was well-liked, after all. People from the shelter, people from a church he attended.

We fill the lunchroom, read scripture, sing hymns, and people share memories of kindnesses Willie had showed them. The most beautiful testifying comes from people in the community, people I'd never heard speak before, old junkies and skittish loners, their words inarticulate and delivered to the floor.

I can't remember what I said. I wish I had written it down.

12.

Sometimes—when I'm heading down Washtenaw, when I'm gliding through Ypsi past the desolate sadness of the midday strip club, past Casino Ken on Prospect, then over toward the train bridge and the sleazy motel, nodding at people I know, everyone doing their best to get by—sometimes I get angry thinking about what happened to Willie. A spiteful and ugly flame kindles in my belly at the thought of those doctors, that pysch, those purveyors of Willie's last humiliation—all except Nurse Dan, who understood and whose compassion was a gift. I think about those criminals who bruised his slender wrists and a bright animal rage warms me. And then, soon, I am forced to consider my own role in the matter—how I abandoned Willie in his final moments, how I failed to understand my responsibilities to him in that most vital instant—and this is a harder thing to look at.

But I try to remember something he told me once. In the car that afternoon, after our trip to Kroger, I asked Willie what happened the day he broke his foot. He was silent for a while as the music played, then his voice got tight with anger.

"That kid who hit me—he was high as hell. He stopped to see I wasn't dead at least, but he was gone, I could see it in his eyes."

We drove on not talking. Then Willie's voice eased, unknit itself. "I guess he was just some scared kid. Knew he coulda went to jail if he stuck around."

The trees blurred around us on Huron River Drive and we caught flashing glints of water through the branches. Even now I can remember how peaceful it was out there on the river. We were on our own little raft away from the world.

"Can't really blame him," Willie said. He sighed and looked over at me. "Gotta have love in your heart, you know?"

A NOOSE IN HENTIESBAAI

(BEFORE)

WE CAME OUT OF THE DESERT and arrived at a small beach town beside the Atlantic. Ellen and I were traveling through Namibia with our two young children and an old friend from Lesotho, where we'd lived on and off over the last few years. Today we had come from a place called Khorixas, Namibia: 245 kilometers across airless flats of sand and rock, baking salt plains that swept cleanly to the edge of vision. As a joke I put on an album by Sigur Rós—I tried to imagine what music represented the opposite of where we were—but the band's glacial Icelandic squalling only amplified the fundamental loneliness of our surroundings. I turned it off. We were on the moon.

Henties Bay felt like a pardon at first—implacable desert for hours, then suddenly a misty beach town materializing from the ether. The town seemed to have fled the desert too, found itself cut off and surrounded by ocean. Pastel houses were shoved up against the Atlantic—purple and blue, yellow, lime, and teal—the colors a rebuttal to the dark churning of the sea. Through coastal vapors we could see baroque alien flora sprouting in defiance of the desert's minimalism. At the edge of the settlement a sign in Afrikaans read Hentiesbaai.

Two things were immediately noteworthy:

The second was a golf course situated in the dried bed of the Omaruru River, composed entirely of sand trap. An archipelago of irrigated green islands ran through the riverbed, punctured by flagsticks that vibrated in the sea breeze.

The first was a noose hanging from a tree near the center of town.

In 1884, Germany began colonizing the area now called Namibia—part of the infamous European "Scramble for Africa"—and the events that followed were predictable and of ample world-historical precedent: the invaders usurped land and resources and occasionally lynched the indigenous people, the indigenous people revolted, the invaders responded with uncompromising brutality. In 1904, twenty years into the occupation, the German General Lothar von Trotha (more dastardly a name than even a dime-store novelist might conjure) was brought in to systematically eradicate the Herero and Nama ethnic groups in the region. "I know enough tribes in Africa," Trotha wrote to the Imperial Colonial Office. "They yield only to force. It was and remains my policy to apply this force by unmitigated terrorism and even cruelty. I shall destroy the rebellious tribes by shedding rivers of blood."

In October of that year, Trotha issued an extermination order declaring that any Herero people (man, woman, child, armed or unarmed) were to be executed if encountered within "German boundaries"—i.e. the southwest corner of the African continent where the Herero had lived for the past three hundred years. The period that followed is now referred to as the Herero and Namaqua genocide, which spanned 1904 to 1908, and which Germany reluctantly acknowledged more than a century later, in 2021, after a six-year negotiation with Namibia over whether what was being offered was officially an "apology" or not. The conflict went like this: after Trotha's colonial soldiers, the Schutztruppe, massacred Herero people with machine guns and artillery, the Germans would chase survivors into the desert, set up a military cordon, and wait for their enemy to become—as one report phrased it—"the victim of his own environment." Most of the Herero people died of starvation or thirst in the interior wilderness; those who didn't escape the cordon were bayonetted or hanged.

Trotha later lightened the tone of his extermination order, instructing his soldiers to shoot over the heads of women and children, an enticement for them to flee into the desert. His intention, he said, was to avoid sullying "the good reputation that the German soldier has acquired"—but in the end Trotha had the women and children executed anyway, some by machine gun, some burned alive in huts. The most haunting accounts from this period come from German settlers and soldiers, who gave sworn testimony about the atrocities they witnessed and participated in. Recent estimates claim that 80,000 Herero (80% of the ethnic group) and 10,000 Nama (50% of the ethnic group) were annihilated over the course of a few years.

It was the twentieth century's first genocide, though not its most notorious. Namibia's first governor, during the prelude to genocide, was Dr. Heinrich Göring—father of Hermann Göring, the man who would found the Gestapo and command the Luftwaffe. In addition to seeking the most efficient means to commit mass murder while avoiding resource expenditure, the Germans in Namibia also fine-tuned the mechanisms of the concentration camp. Captured Herero and Nama people were placed in work camps around the region, where they were subjected to harrowing medical experimentation. The anthropologist Eugen Fischer—later a prominent Nazi—tested sterilization methods on Herero women in the camps and eventually wrote what would become the Nazi's eugenics textbook. At the Shark Island concentration camp—down the coast from Hentiesbaai, near Lüderitz—the German physician Hugo Bofinger also conducted experiments on prisoners, one of which involved injecting arsenic into

Nama men. After the prisoners died, Bofinger would measure brain sizes and ship human remains to the University of Berlin, so scholars there could attempt to demonstrate the similarities between Nama people and anthropoid apes. It is hard not to see men like Fischer and Bofinger as predecessors of Josef Mengele, Auschwitz's Angel of Death, whose experimentation on living prisoners was also aimed at substantiating the biological superiority of the Aryan race.

Most historians resist drawing a bright line between these two German-authored genocides. Others insist on the "uniqueness" and "singularity" of the Holocaust. Whatever the case, certain echoes are uncanny. In their book *The Kaiser's Holocaust*, David Olusoga and Casper W. Erichsen recount how a veteran of the Herero and Namaqua genocide, Franz Ritter von Epp, recruited a young Adolf Hitler into an ultra right-wing militia in 1922. Epp introduced Hitler to many of the future Nazi elite, including Ernst Röhm, co-founder of the thug militia known as the Sturmabteilung (SA). It was through Epp's military connections that Hitler and Röhm were able to outfit their new SA stormtroopers in surplus uniforms from the Schutztruppe—clothing originally intended to camouflage German troops during their ambushes and forays in the Namibian desert. Thus were born the infamous Nazi Brownshirts. Hitler and Röhm clothed themselves in the skins of a previous genocide as they set into motion the next one.

The noose in Hentiesbaai hangs from a perfect natural gibbet: a gray crooked tree, long dead now, with a single branch jutting horizontally. Against the backdrop of the Atlantic the noose falls like a pendant pearl.

At the base of the tree is a marble placard:

THE GALLOWS—ERECTED IN 1978 AS AN APPEAL TO KEEP THE
TOWN AND BEACH CLEAN, INITIATED BY FRANK ATKINSON AND
WILLIE CILLIERS, WHO RESPECTIVELY SETTLED HERE IN 1969
AND 1971 AS THE FIRST TWO RESIDENTS OF HENTIES BAY.

"Jesus," Ellen says. "This thing is from 1978?"
Further up the tree is a rough wooden sign with words carved into
it. I read aloud:
"Absence of discipline—my greatest shame. Frank Atkinson."
She looks over at me. "Where are we?"

In the middle of the twentieth century, a few decades after the
Herero and Namaqua genocide, Namibia experienced a version
of Apartheid, courtesy of neighboring South Africa. It began in
1920, when the League of Nations asked South Africa to take over
administration of Namibia (the Germans had been removed from
power after the First World War). South Africa complied, accepting
a mandate to look out for the "well-being and development…and the
interests of the indigenous population" in Namibia. The League of
Nations referred to this responsibility as a "sacred trust of civilization."

But in 1946, the League of Nations dissolved and Namibia
slipped into political limbo. Rather than grant it independence, as
the international community called for, South Africa attempted to
annex mineral-rich Namibia as their "fifth province." In 1948, the
Afrikaner-led National Party came to power in South Africa and
enacted racist Apartheid policies throughout South Africa and by
extension Namibia. The result was a white minority in South Africa
dictating what neighborhoods Black Namibians could live in, where
they could travel, what jobs they could hold, whether they could vote
(they couldn't), whether they could be murdered without repercussion

(they could)—the list spirals outward along the continuum of human rights violations. With Black Namibians no longer allowed to own property, many were relocated to "reserves." Neighborhoods were bulldozed wholescale. Over the span of just thirty years, South Africa instituted a truly singular interpretation of what constituted the well-being, development, and interests of Namibia's indigenous population.

We stay overnight in Hentiesbaai, having found a pleasant guesthouse by the sea. The town is quiet, mostly empty in the off season. Ellen and the kids run along the beach, dodging waves, trying to shake off the desert's monotony, while Nthabeleng—our friend from Lesotho—sits with me on the deck. We drink fruity cocktails and yell encouragements down to the wave runners. Nthabeleng is a Mosotho woman who has worked as the managing director of an NGO in Lesotho for more than a decade now. For several years she has also been taking classes in her spare time, working first toward a college degree, then an advanced degree. She is between semesters and has come on vacation with us.

After we unpack, I visit the Hentiesbaai tourist website, which highlights some local attractions, the unusual golf course, the excellent fishing. Then I come to an explanation of the noose, which is characterized as a "friendly but firm warning" to keep the beach clean.

"This gesture is typical of Afrikaner humour," the website continues, "seen as such without any negative connotation reflecting on obscure happenings such as real hangings or slavery (which is, by the way, not part of Namibia's history)."

So that's their explanation. Literal gallows humor.

The international community spent decades inviting South Africa to relinquish control of Namibia, but the South Africans declined with regret, again and again. In 1966, the United Nations finally dissolved outright South Africa's mandate to administer Namibia, a decision upheld in 1971 by the International Court of Justice, but South Africa remained unmotivated to cede control. In the meantime, Black Namibians had taken up armed resistance against South African occupation forces.

In 1977, a coalition including Canada, France, the United States, the United Kingdom, and West Germany launched a diplomatic effort to press the point of Namibian independence. The next year, in 1978, the United Nations and neighboring southern African countries urged South Africa to authorize a free, fair, and multiracial election in Namibia to determine the country's self-rule (only whites of European descent had been allowed to vote prior, primarily Afrikaners and descendants of the original German colonizers). Instead, the country held an election marked with "massive organized intimidation by the South African authorities," as the Electoral Institute for Sustainable Democracy in Africa put it. Personal testimonies from this time speak of illegal detentions, confiscated documents, and brutal beatings. The United Nations declared the election null and void and the resulting government illegitimate.

This was the year that Frank Atkinson and Willie Cilliers hung the noose in Hentiesbaai.

To remind people to keep the beach clean.

The next morning we explore the town, which is divided cleanly in half. The lovely pastel beach houses look out at the ocean, nestled on streets with quaint maritime names: Duine, Dolfyn, Pelikaan, Katfisch, Cormoran. On the other side of the main road—away from the Atlantic and pressed back against the desert—is the Black neighborhood. Some houses here are modern, immaculately painted cinderblock with metal roofing, but further back a shantytown emerges: canted structures with clapboard siding and canvas strung over the top, impromptu shelters of metal and tarp, houses cobbled together from car parts and driftwood and other salvaged materials. Here the streets are named after Namibian heroes—Samuel Maharero, Hendrik Witbooi, Iipumbu ya Tshilongo—kings and chiefs who fought the German colonizers around the turn of the last century.

We pass an empty soccer pitch, home to the local team—11 Bullets FC—whose name is painted on the outer wall amidst whorls of colorful graffiti. The field is entirely sand and gravel, with two netless goals bracketing the pitch, and in the noonday sun the stadium appears ready to host the last soccer match of the apocalypse. I stop here to talk with two residents of the neighborhood. A stout chatty man is waiting to pick up his son outside the primary school, passing time with the school's security guard, tall and quiet and eyeing me uncertainly. I tell them I'm traveling through Namibia—from the United States originally but living in Lesotho at the moment—and we talk about the local fishing scene in Hentiesbaai, a topic on which I am comprehensively ignorant.

Finally I get around to my question. When I ask about the noose, the men share a look.

The chatty man shrugs eventually, says, "Ah, it's just some historical thing."

I don't know how to read his avoidance: distrust of a stranger, maybe, or perhaps simply an ingrained reaction to the fact that white faces in this region have been responsible for so much terror for so many years.

I tell the men the noose is an unsettling thing to see in public—it's a symbol in the United States, a threat. This is a bit disingenuous, of course. I don't add, as perhaps I should, that in America we just take a bit more care in concealing our threats, use prettier language. I don't mention that the Confederate Battle Flag—a declaration of intent if there ever was one—fluttered grandly from State of Mississippi flagpoles until deep into the year 2020. I don't tell them how we use the word *reservations* instead of *reserves* like they do in Namibia, don't tell them how when we bulldoze Black neighborhoods we call it *public infrastructure improvement*, don't tell them that when we disenfranchise voters of color we call it *election fraud avoidance*—I could go on and on but don't and don't.

The chatty man laughs uncomfortably. He's just here to pick up his kid from school, didn't pass this way intending to play local historian for some white tourist blowing through town.

"There's no tension here," he says after a moment. "This place is friendly."

We drive back to the tiny commercial strip. In a café there I get talking with a Black woman who's dressed in an ankle-length gray skirt and a serious dark blazer. She's been reading her bible—the pages are highlighted, purples and pinks, greens and yellows, the same pastels as the beach houses. I ask her about Namibia, about Hentiesbaai, and she gives me some local bullet points, sketches out stories that I'll read up on in the coming weeks. Eventually I sidle up to my question about the noose.

"Do you want the official story?" she asks. She repeats the version from the tourist material, the dark Afrikaner joke, the incentive to keep the town clean.

"What about the unofficial?"

A tiny movement of her mouth, hard to classify, perhaps the slightest edge of a smirk, or maybe something more complicated.

"Well, you know this town used to be for whites only—a fishing town, a place for whites to go on vacation. But they had to allow some

Blacks in to do the cleaning, the manual labor, those kinds of jobs." She pauses. "So there are rumors of course."

"About the noose?"

"They didn't like to keep records about those things during Apartheid, did they?"

She tucks in a lavender satin strip and closes her bible.

"But things are different now. In Namibia, Apartheid was not as bad as in South Africa. Blacks here are free, we can go where we please. Some friends I know just moved to the nice houses—" She gestures toward the beach, then stops.

"Their neighbors did move away, but not everyone is like that. Some of the older whites still think that way, but it's smaller now— maybe ten percent, maybe five percent? And if they want to move away, let them."

She places her hand on the bible. "You want to know the truth? We Namibians are Christians. We forgive. It's not how they are in South Africa. The president here, the ministers—we are all born again! We believe in reconciliation."

We sit a while longer, but soon I have to go; we are driving farther down the coast today. I apologize to the woman for interrupting her study and thank her for talking with me.

As I'm turning away, she says, "You know—"

The woman takes off her glasses, rubs her eyes, looks at me.

"—I don't understand why they don't just take it down."

A small shake of her head.

"Someone needs to get rid of that thing."

When we return to the guesthouse to settle up, we are met by the manager of the place, a friendly Afrikaner woman around sixty. She comes to collect the bill, greeting us warmly and doting over our kids, but she doesn't look at or acknowledge Nthabeleng. It doesn't appear spiteful—the Afrikaner woman just seems to think our friend is perhaps our nanny, or maybe something that doesn't require acknowledgement, a piece of luggage, say.

The Afrikaner woman is delighted to hear that I am from the United States. Her son lives there now, she says, in a rural part of Wisconsin, and she begins to wax romantic about the American Heartland.

"It's so safe!" she says. "No danger, no crime—no problems!"

On the way out of Hentiesbaai we pass the surrealistic golf course one last time, where three Black men are out in the sun manicuring those fragmented islands of green, castaways in an ocean of sand. The Namib Desert reasserts itself immediately at the edge of town, the oldest desert in the world, effacing all markers of civilization, and once again everything is whitewashed.

Before we left town I'd grabbed a brochure from the Hentiesbaai tourist office. There on the cover is The Gallows—yet the tree is in silhouette so you can't read the historical placard, can't make out Frank Atkinson's self-flagellating cry: Absence of discipline, my greatest shame!

It's a peculiar image for the brochure cover. It just looks like a picture of a dead tree. The noose has been Photoshopped out altogether.

(AFTER)

THERE'S A STRANGE CODA TO THIS STORY, something that nearly escaped my attention entirely. In autumn of 2020, as COVID-19 seeped into the corners of daily life and the United States roiled in the wake of George Floyd's murder at the hands of the Minneapolis police, someone I knew mentioned they were planning to use my essay about the noose in a class they were teaching. The topic of the course was the power of public images.

I hadn't read the noose essay in years—it consisted of the foregoing material, which was published in 2015—so I returned to the web page to see how the piece held up. When I finished I noticed a comment at the bottom, the first and only note from a reader, submitted by a woman named Petra on June 4, 2020. Curious timing. It intrigued me that someone might stumble into this corner of the internet so many years after the essay had been published.

Mr. McGrath, the note began, and already I was flattered. As a person who spends much of each day semi-nude and staring blankly overtop his computer screen, "Mr." is not an honorific frequently directed my way. But what I had forgotten was that "Mr." also signals the beginning of legal threats and related attempts to speak with one's manager, whether real or metaphorical. I noticed that Petra had a common Afrikaner last name. I read on:

Why do you come to our country and make your own distractions of what happened in our country. We are a peacefull country and you make you own assumptions?? The gallow in Hentiesbay has got NOTHING to do with apartheid / racism, yet you decide you know our country better than we do and write your own story. You heard what you wanted and wished to hear for your great story. You knew you would make money selling a lot of bulldust, no matter what the consequences was. Do you have any idea what you've started in a peaceful country.....no you don't you hipocrate, because in the USA racism is a much bigger problem than here.... remember your

Ku Klux Klan????? And you have the audacity to write a bunch of crap about Namibia and judge us? Please stay out of our country if you can't write something good about my fatherland.

I sat at my desk feeling uneasy. There is a disquieting sensation that arises after spending so many hours of your life writing in the hope of being read, and then realizing that you have indeed been read, and that what you have written while barefoot at your computer has wounded and enraged some invisible unknowable human being on the other side of the globe. I didn't agree with Petra entirely (it was clear that she had, as is the fashion of the internet, not read the article), but she did have a valid point: I had engaged in a kind of parachute journalism, somewhere adjacent to that slimy business practiced most frequently by white men who breeze through foreign outposts filing stories populated with dusky exotics, wholly ignorant of local custom and culture. Who exactly had given me license to write about a place in which I had spent twenty-four hours?

It was Petra's closing thought, however, that left me with a warm queasiness in my stomach. The final line read:

We don't need tourists like you here if the main purpose of your visit is to discredit us and start a racial war, because that is exactly what you did.

I sat in silence. I was unsure what race war Petra was suggesting I sparked. I had no memory of participating in such an event, although perhaps it is precisely that mindset—oblivious, faux-naïf, scrambling for an ill-fitting rag of plausible deniability—that marks the race war participant. But there was something itchily specific about Petra's comment, the timing of it, her use of the past tense (*that is exactly what you did*), and so for the first time in years I googled Hentiesbaai and the noose, and things began to align.

The murder of George Floyd by the Minneapolis police officer Derek Chauvin, on May 25, 2020, ignited a bloom of racial justice activism, an uprising that burned through the United States and across the globe. Early protests centered on police brutality, but the conversation quickly expanded into related issues of systemic oppression—among them the old and recurring question of how we should deal with images commemorating white supremacy and colonial subjugation. How do we disavow without whitewashing? How do we publicly acknowledge our crimes without continuing to do violence?

Within days of Floyd's murder, protestors began to answer these questions in their own idiosyncratic fashion: sculptures of Confederate generals and slave dealers were toppled and beheaded throughout the U.S., as well as in England and in Belgium. Images of Christopher Columbus met a similar fate. University buildings were hastily renamed.

On June 1, 2020, spurred by this rejuvenated movement, two young Black Namibian activists began agitating for the removal of The Gallows in Hentiesbaai. They circulated petitions on Change.org and social media, calling for the noose to be removed and displayed in a museum, where it might be given the appropriate context. These activists issued the Hentiesbaai Town Council an ultimatum: two weeks to consider, or they would take down the tree and noose for them.

One of these petitions cited my noose essay as further reading for people interested in The Gallows' ambiguous history. From there my essay made its way onto Namibian blogs and social media, unbeknownst to me. I assume this is how Petra came to it so long after it was initially published. She left her comment for me a day after the petition made the rounds on Twitter (#TheGallowsMustFall). In autumn of 2020, as I read up on what had been transpiring in Hentiesbaai over the preceding months, I noticed that Petra shared a last name with Frank Atkinson's nephew, who had been quoted in a Namibian newspaper defending The Gallows. It seemed plausible that Petra was another of Atkinson's relatives, had specific lineage tying her to the noose.

For two weeks, the conversation over how to address The Gallows played out in Namibian newspapers and social media. The activists' deadline came and went, with the Hentiesbaai Town Council asking for a weeklong extension, to which the activists agreed. Hentiesbaai has about 5,000 residents, and by this point more than 4,100 people had signed the petition. The town's mayor agreed the noose should go, but asked that the matter be resolved through proper legal channels, which could take time. Then the weeklong extension came and went with no further action. Was it the slow churn of small-town politics? Or the local government's tacit support for symbols of colonial violence? As Petra would tell you, I wasn't there.

Four days later, in the middle of the night, a group of people came to The Gallows and hacked into the tree with axes, then lit it ablaze. The next morning, videos of the burning tree—which still stands, in somewhat mutilated form—circulated on social media. The noose was gone, erased a second time, first through Photoshop, then through fire.

It was unclear how long this second erasure might last.

Nooses aren't hard to come by these days.

HALLUCINATION (DONUT SHOP)

WE FOUND OURSELVES UP IN TIMBER, Sam four, Eve two, the three of
us hung between banks of Maine pine, out on a suspension footbridge
humming like picture wire. The Androscoggin churned beneath us,
engorged with melt, and from the bridge we watched a lost blue oil
drum nod along toward big rocks downriver, where the water tore itself
to shreds, became confetti, a dirty white celebration thrown for these
early days of spring.

We were waiting to see what would happen when that barrel
crested and hit the rocks below—at least that's what I was waiting for,
and I think the children as well, although their minds are veiled at
times. Some part of me hoped for an explosion. It was an oil barrel, was
it not? And oil barrels—this I learned from the action films of the late
1980s—do on occasion explode. I relayed my hope to the children and
they agreed this would be thrilling. We braced ourselves, held breath.
Over went the barrel:

nothing.

Sam sprinted off along the bridge, antelope boy-child, all the
toddler in him burned off very recently, leaving a dusting of new
freckles across his cheekbones and the bridge of his nose. I held Eve
in my arms and we jumped and jumped against the wooden planking,
sending tremors down the line, coded vibrations aimed at Sam, asking

him to please come back, please return so I can feel confident that you will not slip into the charging water and become another lost barrel.

At my thunderous jumping Eve squealed and clung to my neck. Sam returned, older than before, and we left in search of solid ground.

We headed into a mill town whose main street you've seen in the background of underperforming rom-coms or featured on the pages of nostalgic collectible calendars, and there we found a storefront donut shop where we could bivouac for the afternoon. The woman at the register had black black hair and attended to us with a generosity of spirit that felt like a holdover from another vocation—perhaps she had been a happy nun in another life, or a beloved preschool teacher. She was in her mid-forties, first grays starting to fissure her dark hair.

Her hair!—this beyond all else I need to convey: bangs piled into clouds, her hair was a buoyant holdover from the early nineties, hair that predated the tech bubble, hair that predated Enron, hair that had never looted anyone's pension. It was the kind of optimistic hair you ride out a recession underneath. I didn't want to stare in dazed admiration for too long, so I paid for my donuts and coffee and gave Sam a crumpled dollar to cram into the tip jar, an undertaking he performed with priestly solemnity.

This donut shop in Maine was glorious, a vision in burnt sienna, laminate countertops and swiveling vinyl stools—if they were not playing sixties doo-wop then I have overlaid it so in my memory. In the storefront window, the owner had set up a toy kitchen: two plastic ovens, tiny wooden whisks, child-sized aprons stitched with the store's name, and racks of wooden donut simulacra with interchangeable frosting tops. Sam and Eve bustled, serious in bright red aprons, bringing me plate after plate of wooden donuts.

—*Jelly-filled with chocolate frosting: simply divine! But might you*

have a chocolate donut with vanilla sprinkles, and perhaps a maple donut
with raspberry swirl frosting?
—*Right away, sir! Of course, sir!*
They returned to their kitchen and swapped frosting tops, stacked
donuts into careful pyramids. Eve watched Sam, mimicking his
subtle motions. The game lasted for nearly fifteen minutes, a blissful
eternity, and I ate well in that donut shop: two fresh cake donuts, one
chocolate and one apple, dense and moist, no airy yeast donuts in this
establishment. I don't believe they trafficked in that particular kind of
monstrosity. The thought filled me with pride—that the donut makers
and I should be so morally aligned—and I was filled equally with pride
and with donuts.

A woman entered the store. She was in her later sixties, silver hair
chopped at the collar, modestly dressed in a blue-gray pantsuit. This
woman had been watching us through the storefront window for a
while now, I realized, frozen in the street as she observed the rites and
rituals of the children's donut factory. She approached with a hesitant
smile.

"How old is the girl? Is she two?"

"Just under," I said.

The woman and I watched Eve for a moment, grunting to herself as
she baked, dressed in a tiny denim jacket that gave her the appearance
of a tiny Joan Jett. I squinted my eyes and tried to picture her with
punk eyeliner and a Gibson Melody Maker slung over her shoulder,
hair back in a ponytail but strands coming loose and messy in her face,
one tendril stuck finely along a sweat-beaded temple as she stomped in
time to the kickdrum. This reverie filled me with such electric joy that
I had the momentary urge to grab my daughter and squeeze until she
became a fine paste. The circuits in my brain had flooded: the lines for
love and violence run parallel, and the surge of emotion had crossed
the two in uncanny fashion.

"Lovely," the woman half-whispered.

"I'm four!" Sam interposed, putting down a tray of donuts.

Eve heard this and turned, saw us observing. She stretched out her arm in rigid salute, fingers splayed. "Um two!" she yelled, attempting to bend fingers, trying to count her age and not yet succeeding.

"Well," the woman said, and looked at me, her eyes rimming with tears. She was still trying to find the shape of whatever she had come in to tell me.

She left to place an order, then returned a moment later, fidgeting and clutching at the white wax paper bag. The woman was unsure of this whole endeavor now and the smile had left her face.

"The problem—" she said, "—the problem is when they get older."

She tried a smile, but all the warmth had blown off, dissipated on the way to the register. The woman looked haunted, hunted, eyes flitting toward the door like she might run for it, flee whatever silent calamity had visited her hearth. I guessed her to be a bit older than my own mother, so I guessed her children to be a bit older than me. I glanced toward the register but the happy nun was out of sight. We were alone with the woman in the blue-gray pantsuit. Sam and Eve had stopped playing, were watching us now. I became aware that it was very quiet in the donut shop, the needle having skidded from the vinyl.

The woman opened her mouth, girding herself, but didn't speak. Then she left the store without looking at us. Eve raised a hand to her as she passed the window but the woman was somewhere else entirely.

We watched her go. Suddenly I wondered what would happen if we followed. A surreal vision slipped into my head: the three of us trailing behind this woman from innocuous remove, ducking behind hedgerows if she grew suspicious and began to turn, stacking the children onto my shoulders like a human totem pole as we slid into a beech tree's silhouette. I would make a game of it for them, conceal my desperation, winking theatrically and pantomiming broad gestures of secrecy, index finger pressed to lips. We would follow, we had to, but the woman in the blue-gray pantsuit must never know. We would trace her path through the neighborhoods as she worried at the white wax bag, our little caravan progressing toward the edge of town. Soon we'd arrive at a quaint ranch house nestled into pine stand—was there a picket fence? Did she have lawn ornamentation? I couldn't see it yet. But once she was inside, the children and I would creep to the window and peer through the blinds to see what had befallen her. Would she sit on the sofa, face in hands? There must be clues, signposts pointing toward and away. If we looked carefully enough, prepared thoroughly, if we were diligent in our choices, we could learn the ways to neutralize whatever banal mechanisms had cleaved her home.

Through the shop's plate-glass window, I watched the woman turn a corner and disappear. The children continued to play for a while at donut-making and I marveled at how much older they'd grown since we first entered this place. The air in the shop had thickened into something autumnal, cold drafts sliding through invisible seams in the building's foundation. This was an encounter we had in a small mill town along the Androscoggin River, a few miles inland before the coast of Maine ruptures into thousands of Atlantic shards, unmapped islands carried into frigid water.

KEYHOLE TO SANA'A

1.

ONE SUMMER A FEW YEARS BACK, my sister-in-law Maura lost her iPhone in the Hamptons. She was partying at a decidedly retrograde bar in Montauk, The Memory Motel, which is known among the locals as one vertex of the "Bermuda Triangle"—a trio of late-night gin joints where personal dignity tends to go missing under murky circumstances. If The Memory Motel is famous for anything else, it is for inspiring the Rolling Stones' worst song, a seven-minute exercise in yacht rock that bears the same name.

As Maura left The Memory deep into that Saturday night—or Sunday morning?—she realized her phone had gone missing. She talked to bouncers and bartenders who professed ignorance, then had a friend call her phone, which went directly to voicemail. She'd gone out with a full battery, which suggested someone had found the phone and turned it off. When Maura got to her computer later that night she activated Find My iPhone, a service that would send her a GPS-generated map of the phone's location when it next connected to a network. Sunday passed without further information, and Maura returned to Manhattan phoneless.

On Monday morning, Maura received an email from Find My

iPhone. The device had been located: it was currently in Harlem, at the Reverend Dr. Martin Luther King, Jr. Towers, a housing project several blocks north of Central Park. The exact pathways by which her phone had made the 120-mile trek from Montauk to W 112th Street over the preceding thirty-six hours remained unclear, although Maura told me she had a whimsical vision of it making a parallel journey to her own. She started laughing. "Ultimately that phone would've faced the same decisions that any yuppie weekend partier faces: Do you get back by car? Take the LIE? Or is it faster to hop on the Long Island Rail Road?"

As soon as she received the email, Maura called the iPhone from her work phone. It rang once and went to voicemail. When she tried a second time, it was off again. She didn't quite have a plan. If the GPS had given her a more precise location, she said, she might have asked the police to check it out, but in the absence of that, she just thought she'd call up whoever had it and ask for the phone back.

But the phone stayed dark over the next several weeks, and eventually she gave up. Not long after, she took a job in Canada, moved away, got a new iPhone. Maura's life got busy and the whole matter drifted from her mind.

Then, in August, she got another email. Find My iPhone had located the device again: it was in Sana'a, the capital city of Yemen, the mountainous high desert nation that covers the southernmost reaches of the Arabian Peninsula. This is when the pictures began appearing in her iCloud account.

Here's the first picture that caught my eye: an adorable kid in a purple plaid shirt, maybe a little over two years old, with his knock-off Nikes velcro'd onto the wrong feet. He is looking up and smiling at whoever is taking the picture, perhaps the same person who has slicked his hair into a *très chic* hipster side-part—a style that would have fit perfectly in Montauk, except the boy is standing in what appears to be a blown-out bunker, with rubble and wood strewn across the ground, a cinderblock wall in the background, and a dented fifty-five-gallon metal drum lying behind him in the debris.

Next picture: an exterior shot of five buildings—a compound, really—clustered dramatically at the edge of a rocky promontory. The structures are built right up to the point where the rock sheers away into a canyon. The image quality is blurry and it seems the lens has been zoomed in all the way, the picture taken from even higher elevation. The boxy stone and brick buildings are constructed in what I will later come to recognize as a standard Yemeni architectural style.

Now a picture of a man, probably around thirty, dressed in a robe and head wrap, lounging on a mattress: he leans against a bare wall with a satisfied look on his face, his right cheek domed out, stuffed with something. He is frozen in the act of dipping his hand into a pile of qat leaves, which, when chewed, produce "effects similar to cocaine and methamphetamine"—this per the U.S. Drug Enforcement Agency, which classifies one of the plant's active chemicals, cathinone, as a Schedule I drug. A DEA report on qat claims that longtime users can suffer from paranoia, violence, and suicidal depression.

The next picture has no human figures: it is a snapshot of seventeen Kalashnikov assault rifles leaning up against a wall.

Now more pictures of cute kids, two boys and a girl, all under ten. They are playing with an assault rifle, hoisting it over their shoulders, cradling it. One boy of about three stares at the weapon with unguarded admiration, his hand on the stock. A stoic teenager appears in this series as well, resting on his haunches and holding the rifle by its muzzle like a walking stick, crouched with the weary air of a boy soldier returned home from the front.

More than three hundred pictures uploaded automatically to Maura's iCloud once the missing phone came back online in Yemen. There are landscape shots, selfies, internet memes, pictures of dinner, pictures of military and political figures (Syria's murderous tyrant Bashar al-Assad and a pre-execution Saddam Hussein both make an appearance), and scores of photos of an extended family. Many of the pictures involve cryptic images overlaid with lines of Arabic text.

When the pictures of the assault rifles showed up, Maura's family contacted the FBI.

When Maura first showed me the pictures in her iCloud, my ignorance regarding Yemen was complete. Like most Americans, I knew essentially nothing about the country's culture, politics, economy, geography, language, religion, or demographics. As a most basic remedy, I set up a Google Alert for the word "Yemen," something to provide a slow drip of general information while I did some background reading. Over the course of nine months in 2014, Google delivered to my inbox hundreds of articles from news sources around the world—the *New York Times*, *Al Jazeera*, *BBC News*, *Yemen Times*—sketching a rough outline of the country in the process: "Al-Qaeda hotbed," "poorest country in the Middle East," and "terrorist staging grounds" were among the common recurring phrases. The United States had labeled Yemen's Al-Qaeda affiliate the most dangerous branch in the world and was touting President Abd-Rabbu Mansour Hadi and the Yemeni government as essential allies in the fight against terrorism. But Yemen's political leadership was facing its own internal challenges: there was a secessionist movement in the south (the country was only unified in 1990 and had for the preceding twenty-three years been two different nations), a conflict with Houthi rebels in the north, a severe water shortage, frequent blackouts, and a citizenry where more than half the population lived below the poverty line. UNICEF reported that children in Yemen had one of the highest malnutrition rates on the planet. The World Economic Forum, in Geneva, ranked Yemen dead last on its Global Gender Gap Index. And the Sydney-based Institute for Economics and Peace placed Yemen eighth—out of 162 countries—on its Global Terrorism Index. This was the current state of affairs in Yemen, at least according to Google Alerts.

In the meantime, additional batches of photos had uploaded to Maura's iCloud and infiltrated her new phone. She noticed her rarely used Skype account was suddenly filled with unknown Middle Eastern contacts. One afternoon as she planned a trip to IKEA, Maura opened her Notes app to jot down the names of Swedish furniture—Ektorp, Kivik, Malm—and found the notepad already filled with Arabic writing.

At this point Maura began to worry that information of hers might be exposed to the Yemeni users, so she called the help line at Apple. The tech support representative explained that someone had likely installed a new operating system without deactivating the old one or unlinking the device from her iCloud. But there was nothing to worry about, the rep told her, it was amateur-hour stuff, dumb thieves who couldn't see anything of hers. She was looking through a one-way mirror.

Maura and I had become hypnotized by this glimpse into a parallel existence. It was voyeurism at its most basic—simultaneously thrilling and frightening—and like any glimpsed behavior it lacked all relevant context. But we were determined to unravel the story of what had happened to her phone and what it was showing us. I contacted an Arabic scholar I had known for many years and asked her to translate the writing in the Notes app and on the pictures. Maura sought out information about the guns. A family friend identified the weapon the kids are playing with in the pictures: "Definitely a Heckler & Koch HK33," the man wrote, referring to a military-grade automatic rifle capable of firing 750 rounds per minute.

I checked the pictures again. The rifle was equipped with a flash suppressor, which allows the shooter to fire the weapon in darkness.

2.

One evening I met up with the Yemeni comedian Ali Sultan in Minneapolis, where we both live. I'd first heard of Sultan through social media and asked if he would grab a drink with me. I wanted to discuss the iCloud pictures with a cultural native and see what he saw in them. Sultan, who was born in Sana'a and immigrated to the United States in 2003 at the age of fifteen, is a rising star in Minneapolis's comedy scene. Over the last few years he's won comedy competitions throughout the Midwest, performed alongside Kevin Hart and Wanda Sykes, been flown to Dubai to record a special for Comedy Central Arabia, and made his network television debut on *The Late Show with Stephen Colbert*. On stage, Sultan is relaxed and engaging, despite speaking no English when he arrived in the States (his first English word was "always," he says, absorbed from the daytime television maxi pad commercials that served as his early American education). Sultan's success as a performer struck me as particularly noteworthy considering stand-up comedy as a concept doesn't really exist in Yemen. "It's a strange idea to explain to people back home," he told me. "So you stand up and then you tell jokes—okay, so you're a clown? You're in the theatre?"

Sultan's comedy frequently dissects the casual racism that he and others from the Middle East encounter daily in the U.S., but where another performer might indulge in righteous anger, Sultan works in wryly amused mode, his genial and vulpine grin underscoring a wicked intelligence. Jokes from his sets often begin in racially charged territory and then veer unpredictably. One bit has him working at a gas station ("Living the Arab dream," he says, fist-pumping mildly) when a Black customer confronts him over the just-announced death of Osama bin Laden. Yet from this fraught territory the bit swerves into that great preoccupation of young men everywhere: food and its lack. *Maybe,* Sultan muses, as the answer begins to dawn on him, *this is why he and*

his roommate Osama can never get pizza delivered to their apartment,
unit Nine-Eleven.

One October night Sultan and I sat out on the steps of the Acme
Comedy Club, the wind scuttling leaves down the street past us. I
pulled up the cache of images, and when Sultan saw the first picture he
started laughing.

"Okay, you see a lion in the center—a sign of aggression, right?—
and a guy over here with a very serious look, and he's in camouflage and
soldier's boots." Sultan looked up at me. "You know what it says here?
Good Holiday to y'all, and may you be blessed. It's a homemade card for
the end of Ramadan, going to Eid. It's totally innocent, but Yemenis
can be so ridiculous with the Photoshop. This guy in the camouflage is
thinking: I'm the coolest, I just learned how to use Photoshop—put a
fucking lion in the middle!"

Next came images of moody desert landscapes with captions
that turned out to be aphorisms and proverbs and other fragments of
Instagram-ready self-help. *The pain of a heart is not healed by apologies,*
read one line. *Don't partner with a jealous man,* read another. A picture
of a man in a white thawb—the ankle-length robe common in the
Arab world—had a caption reading *Your worthiness is infinite; it is at
the center of my heart.* The man was making the "hand heart" gesture
popularized by Taylor Swift and Justin Bieber.

Many images involved the Yemeni flag—tripartite red, white, and
black—and pictures of the Yemeni flag reimagined as a heart. (There
were lots of hearts.) There were glamour shots of the Yemeni army
standing at parade rest, or leaping into battle, or kneeling in the sajdah
position of Islamic prayer, all set against a backdrop of red, white,
and black. The Yemeni phone users seemed to have the same aesthetic
instincts as the "God Bless Our Troops" bumper sticker aficionados
of the American Midwest. There were several pictures of President
Hadi—America's main ally in the drone war against Al-Qaeda—
looking thoughtful and decisive. But the most striking political images

involved Ali Abdullah Saleh, the former president of Yemen, ousted in 2012 in the wake of the Arab Spring. Someone had Photoshopped Saleh into a series of fervid cinematic landscapes: here was the former president with a superimposed black stallion galloping along a rocky coastline; here was Saleh being hugged by a benevolent leopard; here was Saleh floating beatific over a field, the whole scene framed by a rainbow.

Ali Sultan and I continued to scroll through the pictures, searching for something inflammatory to decode. We came to an image of a blue-eyed Siberian husky sitting forlornly at a computer, his paws up on the keyboard and an Arabic word bubble coming from his mouth. Sultan translated the text as: "Why won't she open her messages?"

He paused for a second. "The dog is at an online dating site."

With the help of Ali Sultan and my Arabic scholar friend, Maura and I were able to piece together a general timeline of what happened to her iPhone. In New York, there exists a robust gray market for second-hand smartphones: some are obviously stolen, sold on street corners and from the trunks of cars; others get passed off as new to naïve customers, wiped and re-boxed with counterfeit user manuals and ersatz "Apple" packaging. Whatever the case was for Maura's device, at some point after July 15, when her iPhone pulsed briefly in the Harlem housing project, a man named Mohammad acquired the phone and updated the Skype profile with his information. Mohammad kept the phone offline and used it as a camera, filling it with selfies from around New York City. One picture features him dressed in a Bulls jersey and a flat-brimmed Rams cap, working at the counter of a bodega. The shelving behind him is a dense Dutch still life of cough syrup, cigarillos, condoms, and cat food. Here now is Mohammad riding an open-roofed tourist bus with the New York

City skyline as backdrop. Here is Mohammad in an army surplus store trying on a WWI doughboy helmet. Here is Mohammad in the bathroom, shirtless, having just edged up his hairline, now sporting a tight chinstrap beard and a sculpted mustache. Perhaps it goes without saying that it is Mohammad who has Photoshopped himself into the arrestingly leonine Eid holiday card, an image he seems to be sending to his young son back in Yemen.

There are Mohammad selfies with sunglasses and without, Mohammad selfies with hat cocked back to the left and to the right. His signature look involves an NFL or NBA replica jersey, but one picture has him in the iconic "I Heart NY" sweatshirt, and another has him wearing a polo shirt with bands of red, white, and black—the Yemeni flag. My favorite is a selfie from the dry cleaners. Mohammad is waiting in line to pick up his newly pressed garments when he notices himself in the full-length wall mirror: purple track jacket, gray sweats, clean kicks, *click*.

Then, on August 2, the first picture from Yemen enters the photostream. It is a shot of a teenager in a white thawb reclining on a couch. Tucked under the boy's woven gold belt is a large jambiya, a curved ceremonial dagger with an ornately decorated hilt and sheath, a symbol of Yemeni manhood. The boy is smiling and sporting a bright red Air Jordan vest over his Yemeni clothing, a picture so perfect—Nike America meets traditional Yemen—that I would have called bullshit had I not seen it with my own eyeballs.

At first it is unclear how the phone has made its way to Yemen. But then, in a picture from August 5, he reappears: Mohammad, selfie king of New York City, resting on a mattress in Yemeni clothing. He dips his hand into a large pile of qat leaves, looking relaxed. Despite the DEA's Schedule I classification, qat is a generally unremarkable substance in Yemen, with qat chewing being an act of communal bonding that has for thousands of years been fundamental to male social life throughout the Arabian Peninsula and the Horn of Africa. "It's a very common practice,"

Sultan told me. "It stimulates you, gets you emotional." The plant produces a buzzy caffeine-like sensation, significantly less dangerous than alcohol or tobacco in terms of addiction. A cynical reader might suggest that the DEA labels certain substances illegal to specifically target and arrest people from, say, the Arabian Peninsula and the Horn of Africa.

Here in his leisure is where Mohammad leaves us. By August 10 he seems to have handed off the iPhone to a teenage relative—a high-end gift, perhaps, from the older cousin who's made it in America. The new owner updates the device under the name "Yacoub"—this is the stoic teen who will later pose with the HK33 assault rifle. Yacoub has flyaway ears he hasn't grown into yet, a wisp of mustache over his lip, and constellations of acne decorating his forehead. I'd put him at fifteen. He rarely smiles but doesn't look unhappy—you can see Yacoub carefully poised on the cusp of adulthood, aiming for some mature stillness. Here he is in farmland outside Sana'a, visiting relatives and snapping pictures of his younger cousins. He gets a portrait of an adorable five-year-old girl, then a picture of her kissing her younger brother on the cheek. Yacoub and the kids pass the phone around, producing pictures saturated with tilted joyous energy: various permutations of hugging relatives, arms slung around shoulders, scenes of easy rapport—and Yacoub, trying his best to look serious while everyone else is smiling.

Flipping through these pictures is like watching Yacoub muddle through adolescence in time lapse. He is deep into the age of identity-building, trying to document and determine his place in the world. He travels through the countryside taking landscape shots from a car's passenger window: stunning mountains with verdant terraced fields, clusters of houses that stair-step down toward a valley floor. Now he is at a construction site looking supercool as he pretends to drive a forklift. Another picture has him posing before a shuttered storefront holding an AK-47 (the gun's safety is on and the stock is folded under so he can't touch the trigger). In late August Yacoub writes the Shahada—the Muslim declaration of faith—in the phone's Notes app, where Maura will discover it while making her IKEA shopping list. *There is no god but God, and Mohammed is the messenger of God.* He writes cheesy love poetry into the Notes app (*How does the heart forget you, the taste of sugar that is lost?*), he tries to visit Sex.com, he takes selfies with qat wadded in his cheek, he is every teenager in the history of teenagers.

One of the final batches of photos comes from a wedding. Yacoub is taking pictures of a nervous groom and a wedding party, their faces all now familiar to me from the photostream. When the wedding party leaves the room, Yacoub steps onto the elaborately decorated dais and takes a series of selfies on the wedding throne, his stoicism still carefully maintained, perhaps envisioning himself one day married. He puffs his right cheek full of air, pretending to have a mouthful of qat, then releases it. As he checks the result on the screen he finds something pleasing there, some intimation of oncoming adulthood maybe, and a sly smile slips across his lips over the course of three quick snaps.

On the steps of the comedy club that October night, I asked Ali Sultan what he thought of the pictures as a whole. He sighed and dragged on his cigarette. "It's just like any of the people I know in Yemen," he said after a while. "This could be my cousin Ahmed. But for the untrained eye—or with what we've been trained to see by the media—it's like: Oh my God, these are fucking terrorists! There's a baby holding a gun!"

So what about the pictures of guns? These, after all, are what spurred Maura's family to contact the FBI. Of the 330 pictures that appeared in her iCloud, about 325 of them are "noteworthy only in their total banality," which is how the Arabic scholar phrased it to me. They are photos of boys watching wrestling or pictures of families surveying their crops or close-ups of hummus and cucumber that would be indistinguishable from any American's Instagram feed.

Let's start with the picture of the seventeen Kalashnikov assault rifles. A closer analysis of the image reveals it to be swiped from the internet, not actually taken by Maura's iPhone. The Kalashnikovs are leaning up against what looks like an American garage door at the end of a paved driveway. It is almost certainly not a photo of Yemen; it looks more like the garage door from my last house.

The pictures of the HK33 are real though. Yet the five photos of Yacoub and his tiny relatives posing with the assault rifle mainly remind me of a picture I took years ago, where I posed with a bristling array of firearms while visiting a gun-owning friend's house. My picture was parody, but parody is meaningless without context. Circulating randomly on the internet, my gun picture would certainly worry some people, the same way I find worrisome the hundreds of context-free pictures and videos of Americans firing their own illegally modified HK33s. YouTube is filled with amateur gun porn like this, with Americans of all ages emptying magazines from illicit full-auto Heckler & Koch weaponry, then turning to the camera and sighing through dopamine grins.

Yemen does have a robust and entrenched gun culture. The Small Arms Survey—an independent research group in Switzerland—ranks Yemen second in the world in terms of civilian gun ownership, with an average of fifty-three guns for every hundred Yemeni citizens. "If you go out in the country," Sultan told me, "they're very into guns. It's like going to the South in America." Particularly in rural areas of Yemen, firearms have become entangled with ideas of masculinity and wealth; an AK-47 strapped across the chest is a status symbol as much as anything.

But no one can do guns better than the U.S.—we are the global leader in civilian gun ownership by a significant margin, averaging one hundred twenty-one firearms for every hundred Americans. So maybe the only conclusion to be drawn from the gun pictures is this: Yemeni civilians have access to heavy firepower just like American civilians. In

America, however, we enact our singular patriotic vision by placing those firearms into the hands of white men who commit massacres at elementary schools, or white men who commit massacres at movie theaters, or white men who commit massacres at country music festivals, or white men who commit massacres at Texas churches, or white men who commit massacres at Walmarts, or white men who commit massacres at Arizona political gatherings, or white men who commit massacres at Colorado high schools, or white men who commit massacres at line-dancing bars, or white men who commit massacres at synagogues, or white men who commit massacres at Florida high schools, or white men who commit massacres at Dayton bars, or white men who commit massacres at Texas high schools, or white men who commit massacres at historic Black churches, or white men who commit massacres at Buffalo supermarkets, or white men who commit massacres at

3.

At the end of September, the pictures stopped coming in. Our access to that world was cut off, our voyeuristic thrill curtailed. Maybe the phone broke, or maybe they got a better operating system overlay. Other possibilities are more troubling. American drone strikes against Al-Qaeda during this period frequently resulted in accidental civilian deaths in Yemen. Maybe some drone pilot in Nevada didn't like the look of that extended family, gathered in their pickups in a tight column, heading toward their cousin's wedding. It wouldn't be the first time we launched Hellfire missiles onto a Yemeni family reunion, won't be the last tragedy born from the assumption that we can understand what we see peering through the digital keyhole.

Then, in the months after the pictures were taken, Yemen slipped first into regional conflict and later full civil war. In March of 2015, Houthi insurgent forces backed by Iran took the capital from the elected Yemeni government, which had been supported by Saudi Arabia, the UAE, and the United States. Since then, Saudi Arabia (using American fuel, intelligence, and munitions) has devastated Yemen with indiscriminate carpet bombing, using the country as a battlefield for its proxy war with Iran. More than 150,000 combatants have died since the outbreak of the war. The civilian casualties are far worse. The breakdown of health services and general infrastructure in Yemen has produced widespread famine and the largest cholera outbreak in recorded history, resulting in the deaths of over 300,000 children. Millions have been displaced. It is impossible to know how the ongoing war has touched Yacoub and his family.

There is another matter I've never been able to resolve concretely. For several months Maura had access to the rivetingly boring daily routines of a Yemeni family near Sana'a. But did they have the same access? The tech support people at Apple told her no, but Maura later noticed one of her new Middle Eastern Skype buddies had changed his profile picture to an image she'd taken—a picture of her husband standing on a rock in Croatia. I imagined a man in Yemen skimming through Maura's photos and stopping at the image of Dan, the Adriatic Sea sweeping flatly behind him, thinking *Beautiful* as he right-clicked "Save image as…" I pictured Yacoub and his cousins crowded around the iPhone, scrolling through shots from the Hamptons. Did they get a peek inside The Memory Motel? What America did they see through the digital keyhole?

There is one image from Yemen that stays with me, a photo someone took of Yacoub. It is late August in 2013 and the war hasn't come yet and the sky is brilliant blue in rural territory outside Sana'a. Yacoub is high above a valley, tiptoed out to the edge of a rocky cliff. The day is warm—he's dressed in a royal blue polo shirt and dark jeans— and there is just open air behind him. The mountains in the distance dissolve into haze and the valley below is lush green patchwork, with trails carving an unknown cursive script through the verdure.

Yacoub faces the camera and sweeps his arm back.

"Look," he is saying. "Come in."

DEATH OF THE VIRGIN

I MET SHANTERIA IN PHOENIX, Arizona, not long before the incident. I had come out to the desert to work at a homeless shelter, a building that was once a meatpacking warehouse and which now served a nightly meal to several hundred people. Each evening the shelter's parking lot filled with wanderers: jumpy addicts, dazed veterans, a woman in angry conversation with her purse, ex-offenders puzzling over their next moves, and men frosted in construction debris, still wearing their plastic knee-guards as they contemplated South Mountain with resigned exhaustion. Some nights there were women and small children in exodus from deadly homes. The district was populated with nomads, people in flight, men and women who slipped across borders or fled the reservation, only to find themselves here, somewhere. The homeless shelter anchored a sunblasted zone of scrapyards and trainyards and it was from this vantage, at the center of the city, that we watched the sprawl of Phoenix leak out into the Sonoran Desert. Even the city was headed elsewhere.

I only talked to Shanteria once and never saw her again. She was tall, with long beaded braids hanging halfway down her back, heavy beautiful cords that swung languidly as she entered the room. Shanteria carried herself with the dreamy grace of someone moving underwater.

I called her name off the list, mispronounced it, and she corrected me gently.

"It's Shan*ter*ia, honey," she said. "But everyone says it wrong."

She was at the shelter that day to use the office phone, calling her daughter in Baltimore. My job required me to dial the number and wait in the small room until she was done with her call, since things tended to disappear when the office was left unattended. I busied myself shuffling through the desk and rearranging the bulletin board, but it was meager theater; eventually I leaned back in the chair and stared at the ceiling. This incursion into her personal life seemed to bother me more than it did Shanteria. She was well accustomed to the myriad minor humiliations of homeless living.

On the other end of the line, I could hear a tiny cheerful voice chattering away. Shanteria had called to see what her daughter thought of the third grade. For most of the conversation she smiled down at the desk, but one time she looked up at me, grinning, shaking her head at some bit of hilarity taking place in Baltimore, wishing she could share the joke with someone. After a brief conversation she hung up and thanked me for the use of the phone. Her long beaded extensions slapped against the metal doorframe on her way out.

Shanteria worked as a prostitute in our neighborhood. She was somebody's daughter, somebody's mother. She was murdered in early October, just as the heat was beginning to let up.

Alex is Shanteria's boyfriend. Such a strange word to use—boyfriend—but that's how he phrased it, like he was going to take her to prom. Alex spends his days breaking concrete at a construction site, his nights down here beside the shelter, getting high and blacking out on an old bedroll he hides in the bushes while he's at work. His drug of choice is crack cocaine, Shanteria's too, but he dabbles in heroin and alcohol when the opportunity presents itself.

Alex is lean, pared down to essential elements. The muscles of his arms ride densely along the bones—his skin is shrink-wrapped—with veins that traverse his forearms and root themselves in the backs of his hands. His eyes are deep in hollow bowls, his cheekbones hatchet-cut. Some days Alex responds when I see him in the street and say hello, and some days he does not. He rarely laughs and it seems like the wrong word will tip him into sudden violence. He greets my jokes with silence: he doesn't think they're funny, and, as the words leave my mouth, I don't think they're funny either.

This is a later memory of Alex, after I've known him for a while:

There is commotion outside the shelter. I hear yelling and follow a trail of blood spatter through the parking lot, out into the street, where a small crowd is gathering.

Two drunks fighting, they tell me. Got them separated and they went off in opposite directions. Then one turned and hit the other guy in the back of the head, cracked his skull against the pavement.

The man is lying on the ground, unconscious and bleeding from his forehead, pants pissed. I'm trying to clear space around him but everyone is shouting advice, crowding in, everyone has an opinion.

Then Alex is beside me.

"Everybody step back now."

Alex does not yell but his tone will not accommodate any alternatives. We all step back.

"Get me two wet clean rags," he says to me. "Clean, understand? And call an ambulance."

By the time I return Alex has rolled the unconscious man onto his side. He sweeps the man's mouth clear with his first two fingers. Blood and saliva ribbon onto the ground. Just beyond the circle of people I can hear dogs thrashing against a chain link fence, barking and scrapping in the dirt, this wild clamor coming from the next property where a puppy mill operates behind tall barriers. It sounds like hundreds of frothing animals smashing against the fence.

Alex strips down to his tank top, carefully makes a pillow from his dark blue work shirt, and places it under the unconscious man's head. He takes the rags from me and swabs the man's forehead, then presses one to stanch the flow of blood. His fingers brush lightly across the man's skin, as if he is smoothing out a delicate piece of parchment. Then Alex takes the man's hand and starts talking.

"I want you to squeeze my fingers. Little squeeze."

The man's eyelids are twitching.

"That's right, come on now. Let me see it."

A nearly imperceptible tightening. A slight wriggle of the fingers.

Suddenly the paramedics have arrived to take control. The crowd disperses quickly—no one sticks around once the authorities are on the scene—and after another moment the man begins to come around. I tell the paramedics what happened and then look for Alex. He's already halfway down the block, walking quickly. I jog after him.

"Hey, I wanted to say thanks."

Alex stops but does not turn around.

After a moment he speaks. His voice is hard.

"The only way to stop this—"

He turns and looks at me, sweeping his hand broadly toward the encampments along the street.

"—the only way to stop this bullshit—"

He is livid, tries to collect himself.

"All this trash? All these subhumans out here? They need to be executed."

His fists are clenched and pulsing.

"We've gotta take all these subhumans and put them against a wall and execute them."

Then Alex continues down the street.

But as I said, this is a later memory of Alex. This happened a few months after Shanteria was murdered. Alex had committed himself fully to the desert's nihilism by that point. Sometimes I try to remember he wasn't always so angry.

Alex reminds me of some paintings by Caravaggio. I couldn't have told him this—he would have hated it, would've sneered at the thought there was anything beautiful in him—but it was true. For a while it eluded me, but the day I watched him minister to that drunk in the street, bent over in his sweaty tank top, his junkie laborer's body in fluid attention—a pathway lit up in my brain. It was only after I found a book of color plates in the library that I was able to confirm it.

In Caravaggio's painting *The Entombment*, it is the powerful right arm of Christ, slipped loose and dangling, cold fingers brushing against stone as his disciples struggle with the awkward weight of a corpse. In *The Martyrdom of St. Matthew*, it is the arm of a young assassin who has just run his sword through the fallen saint, the same arm now cocked and ready to stab again. It's there in *Judith and Holofernes* too, the tyrant's arm clutching at bloody bed sheets while Judith slits his throat, and it's there in *The Crucifixion of St. Peter*, the old man's arm flexed and straining, already pinioned to the wood, as the grizzled martyr is hoisted and hung upside down. All those arms are Alex's arms.

Caravaggio was a dirty realist, uninterested in the idealized bodies and precious triangular compositions of the painters who came before him. His commissioned altarpieces were often rejected for lacking propriety, filled with spurting arterial blood, grimy fingernails, and the worn and muddy feet of saints and peasants alike. He used physical laborers and prostitutes for his models, and he would have been captivated by Alex's sinewy earthbound body.

And Alex would have recognized Caravaggio as well. The painter was one of the most notorious denizens of early seventeenth-century

Rome: frequently caught fighting in the street, responding to insults with sudden violence, in and out of prison, a fixture in the Ortaccio— the "evil garden"—the neighborhood tucked beside the Tiber where prostitutes were required to live. Some contemporary art historians claim Caravaggio was a pimp as well as a painter, which might account for the number of prostitutes that modeled for his canvases. His St. Catherine, his Judith, his repentant Mary Magdalene—these female heroes of Christianity were all well-known Roman prostitutes, women that Caravaggio rendered with tenderness and humanity, women he surely loved in some way. This too Alex would have understood.

Here's how I heard:

Alex finds me in the shelter parking lot one evening. People are lined up alongside the building, waiting for dinner to start, and I'm about to begin passing out paper plates and calling people inside. Boxcars rumble toward Albuquerque and then the Great Plains. Beyond the switchyard, South Mountain watches over us in serene deistic remove. Night is coming gradually and up and down the block people have staked their claim, laid out seam-popped sleeping bags and ratty blankets. From the end of the street comes the lilting muted sound of someone playing Mexican folk songs on an acoustic guitar.

No, it isn't Alex who finds me there but something Alex-shaped, something emptied out, a form filled with air. He is talking to me but staring past me, his eyes glassy. At first I assume he is high, and maybe he is.

"Shanteria's dead," he says. "I hadn't seen her for days. Then they found her in the alley."

His face is blank: not angry, not sad, not anything.

"She was carrying my baby," he says. "I never told you that."

I open my mouth but don't say anything.

"Found her in the alley, now they're both gone."

Then Alex too is gone for a while. About a week later, I see him lined up for dinner. His left eye is domed out like a ripe plum, his face cut up, the skin peeled away in patches. It looks like he's been dragged through the street. But he is present, not the phantom of last week.

I ask what happened to him.

He looks at me with forced thoughtfulness, like he's going to say something philosophical, introspective, like he's speaking from some place of inner calm—but from the way he's holding his body it seems like his insides are jagged and tangled, shot through with jangling bolts of electricity.

"That night I learned about Shanteria I went out looking to die. I decided I would go see her, go meet my baby. But I couldn't do it myself so I went to get killed."

He licks his wounded lips.

"I knew who would do it, though." Alex says the name of a local dealer, a man whose ominous presence blows occasionally through the neighborhood like a passing thunderhead. "I found him out in the street with his people, walked up to him and hit him in the face. I called him a jail bitch, called him a punk faggot, and then I waited for it."

Alex stops, wants to see if I have anything to add.

"That dude stomped me out. Him and his boys had me on the ground, kicking me—and I begged them to keep going."

The heat is pressing down as Alex talks, no relief even with evening coming.

"Finally he took out his knife, put it against my throat. I begged him, but he wouldn't do it. Just left me on the curb."

People are heading in to eat, moving past him in line now, but Alex doesn't notice.

"When I came to, I was in a hospital bed. I decided God himself had stopped that blade. But it don't feel like another chance. Just feel like punishment."

There is a painting by Caravaggio called *The Death of the Virgin*. The work was intended as an altarpiece that would depict the final moments of Mary, the mother of God, before she ascended into heaven. When Caravaggio delivered the piece in 1606 it was almost immediately rejected by the nuns who had commissioned it.

The official reasoning given was his raw treatment of the scene: Mary's body lies splayed on a table, lit from above, pale and very dead. Her left arm sticks out toward the viewer, hand hanging at the wrist, and her bare feet are already starting to stiffen. Mary Magdalene sits beside the body, folded in exhaustion, and John the Evangelist stands behind her, hand on his cheek, staring mournfully into space. Other disciples are gathered around in darkness, wiping away tears, hands over eyes, everyone silent and stunned and grieving. Mary is not ascending into heaven, and these are not people who look hopeful for a resurrection. It is a scene of personal devastation, recognizable human mourning over a beloved friend.

The other major objection to the painting was that Caravaggio modeled the figure of the Virgin Mary on a prostitute he loved. This too was insupportable. The woman in the picture is far too young— Mary would have been nearly fifty—and she is tragically beautiful in death. Her right hand rests on her stomach, which is swollen in what appears to be the early stages of pregnancy, a supposed allusion to Mary's sacred motherhood.

All of this was too much: a dead pregnant prostitute had no place over the altar. The nuns eventually found a suitable replacement for the rejected work, another version of the Virgin Mary's death, done by Carlo Saraceni. In his painting a beatific Mary rises through cottonball clouds while pink cherubs pluck harps and violins. They are waiting to crown her with flowers.

It took a few months, but they did catch the man who killed Shanteria. He currently resides in the maximum-security Central Unit out in Florence, where someday off in the future the Arizona Department of Corrections will transport him to the death house next to Unit 8 and execute him by lethal injection.

Cory Morris—a man who worked as a DJ in a dive bar a few blocks from the homeless shelter—murdered Shanteria and four other women in the neighborhood, left their bodies in an alley a few blocks from where I was living at the time. After the police arrested Morris, they began checking into places he had lived previously and found a string of similar murders in Oklahoma; no one knows exactly how many women he killed. As I came to his mugshot I realized I had seen him before in that dive bar. He sat behind the turntables, thick and impassive, with a tidy mustache and goatee, the expression on his face unchanging as he spun cuts from George Clinton and Parliament-Funkadelic.

Here's how Morris operated: he identified vulnerable women in the neighborhood and took them back to the small trailer where he slept, out behind his aunt and uncle's house, enticing them with offers of money or drugs. In each instance, Morris had sex with his victim, got her high, and then strangled her—sometimes with a necktie, sometimes with the nylon strap from a gym bag. Several times he kept the body in his trailer for days, slept beside the corpse, before eventually dragging it out to the alley.

One can only marvel at the time and energy the Phoenix Police Department invested in the deaths of these women. Four of the women's bodies were dumped about fifteen feet from the back gate of

Morris's yard—some of them just weeks apart—and court documents describe drag marks leading toward his back gate, as well as signs that the gate had been removed from its hinges and then rehung. Yet for seven months these murders went unsolved—a standard case of NHI, as a cop once phrased it to me, No Human Involved. The value of life varies from district to district in Phoenix, and a dead pregnant prostitute doesn't provoke much in terms of civic urgency. It was the uncle who finally figured it out, who opened the trailer door one day while Morris was away, drawn back there by a terrifying odor.

Cory Morris later admitted that he lured Shanteria to his trailer with the promise of five dollars. He had sex with her and then strangled her with her long beaded hair extensions. I can only pray that she was already high, already drifting away from this world, up through the cottonball clouds.

After *The Death of the Virgin* altarpiece was rejected, Caravaggio began a rapid slide into disarray and entropy. About a month later he killed a man, a pimp with whom he had a longstanding grudge. They famously dueled on a tennis court and Caravaggio stabbed the pimp in the groin, sliced open his femoral artery, and the pimp bled out. The painter then fled Rome and joined the Knights of Malta, an order that provided papal dispensation from the death sentence that now hung over his head. But Caravaggio found no stability there either: a year into his stay on the island he assaulted a high-ranking knight, seriously injuring him, and was expelled from the Knights of Malta as a "foul and rotten member." He was thrown into prison, vulnerable once again to anyone who wanted to collect the bounty on his life.

No one quite knows how it was managed, but Caravaggio escaped from jail. He had been imprisoned in an underground rock-walled cell on Malta, surrounded by castle ramparts that dropped two hundred feet into the sea. Then: vanished. A few days later he resurfaced in Sicily—having covered fifty miles of open water—where he hid out with friends in Syracuse, then Messina, then Palermo. He made it up the mainland to Naples before his debts caught up with him. There in the Cerriglio, a brothel known for catering to pansexual appetites, three men ambushed Caravaggio and pinned him to the ground, while a fourth man slashed his face, gave him the mark of sfregiato—a revenge attack likely orchestrated by the injured knight from Malta.

Caravaggio lived another few months, hunted and wandering, significantly disabled from the sfregiato, in and out of jail again. He made it to Porto Ercole, where he was dreaming of a pardon and a return to Rome. He died there in exile. Some claim he was assassinated, but the more likely explanation was heart attack. He was thirty-eight years old.

Alex is in exile too. Now that Shanteria is gone I don't see him associating much with other people. He lives in some interior world. He goes to work, breaks concrete under the Phoenix sun, gets high, passes out beside the shelter. His face is a stony mask and sometimes he talks to me about Shanteria and sometimes he talks about executing the subhumans, tells me how everything out here is trash.

But I saw him that day, not too long ago.

I saw how tenderly his hands moved. I saw how he made a pillow from his dark blue work shirt.

HALLUCINATION (ACTIVE SHOOTER)

THEY LOCKED THE DOOR AND CUT THE LIGHTS. We stood in darkness, breathing.

In the hallway, a woman's voice intoned from the community college's public address system, offering guidance on how we should avoid death. *Please seek shelter immediately*, she said. The emergency lights pulsed in sharp silent bursts. *The doors will lock electronically. Please move away from windows and silence your phones.* Her voice was a balm.

The young man in the dark beside me was unable to speak quietly. I recognized it as behavior I had witnessed in my children. "What I don't get—" he said, and someone shushed him. His voice was monstrously loud in the enclosed stillness. He tried to lower it for a moment, but the volume returned almost immediately, unbidden. "I don't get why we practice this. So we can show all the good hiding spots to the shooters?" My ear snagged on his use of the plural—*shooters*—as if he carried in his head some dark foreknowledge. A few minutes earlier, this young man had been in line behind me while I bought an iced coffee from the kiosk down the hall, his round sallow face, his wisps of red beard along the jawline. He'd tried out a variation of the same comment then, when the emergency system engaged, but people were already drifting off in confusion, and there was no audience to appreciate his cleverness.

A woman had waved us into the Development Office as we

wandered down the hall. "You can't be out here," she said, corralling loose students and people who didn't have classrooms to shelter in. A middle-aged Somali woman in a floor-length black jilbab passed the doorway and the Development woman diverted her inside. "I am studying for my exam?" the Somali woman said, mildly worried.

"This is just practice," the Development woman said and pulled the door shut.

We moved into an inner room. We were in the Development woman's personal office now. I could see a picture of the woman and her husband taped to her computer monitor—*Barcelona, maybe?*—but then she snapped the light off and I couldn't see anything. The iced coffee was slick and condensing in my hand.

After a period of silence, a female student whispered, "My mom always told me never to give anyone the finger while I'm driving." I was listening to the differences in character of people's breathing. "So I don't get shot," she said. I could hear people in the room smile uneasily, ejecting little puffs of air through their nostrils.

I started tapping drum triplets against the coins in my pocket, but the sound was jarring, outsized, and I could feel people turn to look at me. I tightened my fingers into a fist. The Somali woman shifted her books from one arm to another. "This is like when they wouldn't have electricity over there," she said softly, floating back toward some childhood memory that predated the Somali civil war.

Earlier in the week, an administrator had sent a chipper note of preparation to the staff. *Hello everyone and HAPPY WEDNESDAY!! Just a friendly reminder that one week from today will be our active shooter drill.* Attached to the email was a PDF—a "quick reference guide" it was called—as if the candlesnuffing of our physical existence might benefit from an index or glossary.

The quick reference guide began with a definition: *An active shooter is an individual who is engaged in killing or attempting to kill people in a confined and populated area.* It reminded me of essays in the freshman comp classes I taught at the community college. *Webster's Dictionary defines "culture" as the social customs of… Merriam-Webster classifies a bump stock as an illegal modification to a semi-automatic…* When those flat ugly cracks of gunfire began in the hallway, in the classroom, we could consult our quick reference guides to determine whether the event met the definition or fell just short.

Embedded in the email was a video. The screen opened black, clouded with ominous ambient music, then sharp reports of rifle fire punctured the stillness. The video bore the off-brand production quality of an old episode of *Rescue 911*. A series of law enforcement figures narrated grainy reenactments of campus shootings. They were uniformly beefy and sun-pinkened, a parade of bullnecked white men with Oakleys perched atop their heads, just so, as if modeling a line of matte black tiaras.

These men confronted us with the decision-making tree of an active shooter event: run or hide or fight. They seemed most excited by the final option, but perhaps I was imagining this. *You will have to become more aggressive than you ever imagined*, the men said. But they were already subtly disappointed in us, knew we were unprepared for the enormity of our mortal encounter. They had resigned themselves to our softness. *Total commitment and absolute resolve*, one of the thick men said, and I knew he meant we should picture ourselves murdering the active shooter so to avoid being murdered, so to prevent more murder from transpiring. If the endless stream of business self-help books has taught us anything, it is that visualization is the key to achieving our dreams. The last section of the video discussed how to improvise weapons from our tools of education; the shaky cam reenactment depicted students hurling textbooks and backpacks at the gunman. I wondered if I'd be able to wrestle the man to the ground. Would I then push my thumb into the firm jelly of his eye socket? Or would I, with book or boot, smash and smash until I felt a caving? Through what precise alchemy would I render the active passive?

We stayed in that inner room for a while, disembodied, listening to the intimate shifting and repositioning of our physical selves. A unit of time passed that was the exact shape of human breathing. Then the woman's gentle voice began issuing from the intercom again, informing us the drill was complete.

In the hallway I passed the coffee kiosk and the two Spanish-speaking women who ran it. One of the women was almost entirely bald, her remaining strands of hair pulled across her bare scalp into a thin ponytail. The other woman was very round. The most prominent characteristic of these two women was their extreme cheerfulness, which expanded like a soap bubble, wobbling and enclosing the kiosk in a shimmery gloss. These two women were beloved by the students, who frequented the kiosk seemingly with the primary intention of practicing their rudimentary Spanish phrases. The more adventurous students attempted gerunds, honed imperfect tense constructions. I frequented the kiosk with the primary intention of spying on these interactions, from which I derived a great warming sensation of the potential for human good.

"Hola, chica!" the very round employee called out to a young Somali woman, who grinned and in return floated onto the river of the day a Spanish phrase she had just learned in class, then squinted uncertainly, waiting to see if the phrase would bob along or capsize under its own balkiness. The employee laughed and tweaked an aspect of grammar, then rung up the student's purchase. Several minutes prior, the two women who ran the coffee kiosk had been hiding in the mute darkness of an adjoining supply closet. They struck me as the inverse of the beefy men from the active shooter video, who asked us to gird ourselves for violence, who taught that the inevitability of violence can only be countered by our own violence, that we must multiply violence by violence to set in motion an equal or overwhelming response.

When I was almost back to my office, I saw Jerome, one of my freshman comp students, a queer Black man in his mid-twenties. Jerome arrived fifteen minutes late to each class, disheveled and sheened in sweat, and addressed me unfailingly as *Professor* when most students simply called me *Will*. In the last week Jerome had been hard at work on his persuasive essay, which attempted to make the case that the capital-m Media wasn't giving President Trump his due, that the president was actually more benign than the MSM made him out to be. Jerome's research had so far consisted of tweets he summarized in his body paragraphs. When I pressed him after class one day on Trump's bad faith interactions with the LGBTQ community, Jerome admitted he sometimes felt troubled by what he overheard—but then wondered if it wasn't just another case of the Media misrepresenting the president's true beliefs.

Jerome widened his eyes as we passed. "Professor, you survived!"

I shook my head at the strangeness of it and asked where he'd taken shelter.

"I got to join some World Politics class."

I thought for a moment to make a lighthearted reference to his Trump paper but didn't want to seem like I was teasing him, so instead we chatted with the awkward jauntiness of two people who had recently been forced to consider the termination of the self.

As we made small talk, I wondered what would happen if the gunshots began now. Or now. These events usually lasted less than two minutes, from first trigger-pull to last. Would we run, I wondered, or stand in confusion. What if they began now. Would Jerome and I huddle in a classroom, shove a desk against the door. Would we make eye contact as we lay belly down on the linoleum or would we stare through the floor. Would we cry, the both of us grown men, would we hold hands. It felt shameful to consider how pathetic I might appear in those final moments, weeping and bloodied, and then more shameful still that my personal vanity had factored into this terrible equation. Would I grab the smoking barrel as it nosed into the classroom, and would it burn my hand, or would the adrenaline and terror prevent me from registering the sear of flesh. And how hot are the bullets when they enter, and can you feel a tearing in the abdomen, a wet ripping, or is the sensation more like blunted impact, a series of blows from a baseball bat. Would I charge the active shooter, as I've told myself I must, accept my fate in motion, or would I freeze and beg mercy: *Please, you don't understand, my kids will be waiting at the bus stop, that was our arrangement.* And will they be confused when I don't show. Will they drift in mild befuddlement to a neighbor's house, the fourth-grader's arm around his little sister's shoulder—a twinge of excitement even, something different today, something unusual. And will Sam practice his least common denominators, practice slurring notes on the violin. And how will I tell Eve about the poodle I saw, I'd meant to tell her at breakfast, if only she could have seen: full winter and on the highway a man was driving a white painter's van, ladders on the roof, driver's side window rolled down. He passed me doing seventy. The man had white hair, was in a dirty white undershirt in a white van in full winter, dragging on a cig. Small white clouds of smoke tufted from his window, and unperturbed on the man's lap perched a white poodle, head regal and alert, fur ruffled in the wind, that poodle gazing out across the lone and level tundra, master of all he surveyed.

EXCAVATIONS

PEANUT'S ODYSSEY

1.

CLIFF JONES HAS LARGE EXPRESSIVE EYES, milky brown and roaming. They are at any moment liable to narrow in defiance, widen in amazement, rim with tears, or mellow into pensive stillness, watching you, listening, always watching. When he makes a point he'll place his index finger at the corner of his eye—*You've gotta see what's really going on*—and hold your gaze unblinking. He is attuned to quick movements on the periphery, a bearing honed across decades of incarcerated living. "Prisons thrive on confusion," Cliff told me. "Every day, you don't know what to expect. Am I going to see somebody get killed? See the guards beat somebody up? Will I get into a fight?"

One bright January day Cliff took me through his old neighborhood in New York, near 107ᵗʰ and Central Park West. We were heading for the scene of the crime. This was nearly two weeks into the new year and the Christmas trees of the Upper West Side lay heaped and browning along the sidewalks. Cliff, who was sixty-three at the time, is tall and thin and moves with the unstudied grace of someone who grew up gliding across the basketball courts of Manhattan and the Bronx, and later those of the New York State Department of Corrections, where for nearly thirty years he was Inmate 81-A-3316. Cliff is internal and alert, a man who hums along at low RPMs before accelerating into righteous vindication or sudden enthusiasm. As we strolled the neighborhood he would occasionally spot a familiar sight—the wall where he used to play handball, or the corner where his friend's older sister taught him to ride a two-wheeler—and break into a beneficent smile, a gift made powerful by its scarcity.

In 1981, Cliff was convicted of rape, murder, and attempted robbery. Following his release from prison in 2010, he had been living in the Bronx and had become an infrequent visitor to his old Manhattan neighborhood. As he reacquainted himself with the area, his eyes were in constant scan. Then, on 107th Street, we ran into a man in his thirties who was chatting with friends in front of an apartment building. "Peanut!" the man called out happily, then dapped up Cliff, and I watched his demeanor begin to loosen. This was the son of one of Cliff's oldest friends.

"You walking with a great man," the son told me. "A standup brother." He ducked inside the apartment building, insisting we follow. "Ma, I got a guest for you!"

Suddenly Cliff was coy and joking. He tapped on the doorframe of one of the first-floor units and poked his head inside. "Is Ms. McCallester here?"

A woman in her sixties came rushing from the kitchen and wrapped Cliff in a bearhug. She introduced herself as Ruth Anne and began clearing space for us in the sitting room, which was forested with old basketball trophies, CDs and cassettes in dusty towers, pictures of her children on the walls. "We've been friends since the third grade," Ruth Anne told me, then dipped into the kitchen and returned with shot glasses of Patron, a corrective to the January chill. "But he don't tell me nothing," she teased. It had been a while since they'd seen each other. "He got his little girlfriend, so he don't talk to me anymore."

Cliff tried to interject but was overruled.

"I'm sorry—he is so in love!"

In the sitting room Ruth Anne told me how hard it was to comprehend Cliff's thirty-year disappearance into the carceral system. When he'd been accused, in October of 1980, of raping a woman and murdering a male bystander in the crime's aftermath, Ruth Anne was certain it was a mistake that would quickly be resolved. "He just wasn't that kind of person," she said. "How do you get a killer out of a Peanut?"

As we sipped tequila on the couch, Ruth Anne told childhood stories about Cliff and tales of neighborhood cookouts in the years following his release. She patted his leg proudly. When Cliff mentioned she had written a character letter for one of his many parole appeals, Ruth Anne's eyes lit up. "You want me to read it?"

She booted up the ancient Dell in the corner of the sitting room and began to read aloud. Her letter described a kind and respectful boy beloved by the neighborhood mothers, one of four smart, athletic brothers who avoided the corners and represented the neighborhood well on the city's basketball courts. The Cliff Jones she had known for decades was a gentle and generous soul, robbed of his promise by charges unfathomable to her.

"I love Peanut, as I call him, as a brother," Ruth Anne's letter concluded. "I know him to his core and I know he could never have taken another life. He is very much loved, and we don't even see the crime he was burdened with. We know Peanut too well to even consider it." Throughout her recitation Cliff sat on the couch staring into his lap, silent and stoic.

After a moment I asked where the nickname Peanut came from, and Ruth Anne said her husband came up with it. She looked over at Cliff.

"Because you got that peanut head!" she said, laughing, and finally Cliff cracked a smile. "That's what it is!"

Some things were never in question. On June 2, 1980, a man raped Leona Robinson on the fourth-floor landing of an apartment building near 104th and Columbus, three blocks from where Cliff grew up. Robinson was a local sex worker who had gone into the building with a potential john before getting skittish. When she attempted to back out of the transaction the man raped her at knife point. As the assailant fled down the stairwell he encountered Ramon Hernaiz, a sixty-two-year-old resident of the building, who was helping his elderly mother-in-law carry groceries to her apartment. As Robinson called for help from above, the assailant grappled with Hernaiz and then stabbed him several times in the back with a steak knife, puncturing his spleen and kidney. While Hernaiz lay bleeding, the assailant rooted through the dying man's pockets, stole his wallet, and bolted. When police officers interviewed Robinson, first at the crime scene, and then later that evening in the hospital, she gave a detailed physical description of the assailant, whom she interacted with, in her telling, for at least fifteen minutes in clear light.

Months passed with no substantial leads and the detectives assigned to the case grew eager to resolve it. In 1980 the NYPD was contending with its worst year of murder, robbery, burglary, and theft since the department had started keeping numbers back in the 1930s. So in late September, Detective Michael Holland, a fifteen-year veteran of the force, called Robinson back into the precinct and directed her to look at a photobook of people who had been arrested in the area in previous years. It was at this time, nearly four months after the crime, that Robinson first identified Cliff. His picture was in the photobook due to his sole arrest, in 1977, for a misdemeanor drug charge. Cliff had spent sixty days on Rikers Island and had no further run-ins with the police. There were two issues with Robinson's photobook ID, however: the first was that she was high on heroin when she picked Cliff's photo, which Detective Holland knew at the time and which Robinson later confirmed in court; the second was that the photo of Cliff in almost no ways matched the description Robinson had given at the time of her attack. The question of the assailant's and Cliff's physical characteristics would become further muddied during the ensuing trial, but the main point of overlap was that both were Black men.

The police began looking for Cliff, but he no longer lived in the neighborhood where the crime had occurred. For the previous several years he had been staying with his mother in the Bronx. Weeks passed. One day a friend told Cliff that detectives had come by asking questions about him, but they wouldn't disclose anything further. "I didn't pay it no mind," Cliff told me. Several more days passed and the detectives reached Cliff's older brother, Kenneth, and said they wanted to talk with Cliff. Certain of his brother's innocence, Kenneth convinced him they should go down to the precinct together and clear up the misunderstanding. On October 25, 1980, the brothers walked into the 24th Precinct on the Upper West Side. Cliff Jones would not see another day of freedom until a decade into the twenty-first century.

At the precinct, Detective Holland questioned Cliff about the rape of Robinson and the murder of Hernaiz. Cliff said he'd never heard of either of them. When Holland asked Cliff where he had been that day in June, which was now five months prior, Cliff suggested he might have been helping a friend lay flooring, but couldn't produce a solid alibi. He spent his days doing odd jobs or playing basketball, which he'd been paid to do since he was seventeen, when an older friend recruited him to a team of ringers who hustled on courts around the city. Holland then asked Cliff to stand in a live lineup. From behind a two-way mirror Robinson identified Cliff as the perpetrator; moments later, he was in handcuffs. Kenneth rushed off to rally the family, hoping to raise bail, but they were unable to muster the funds. Cliff was transferred to the Tombs for booking and then to Rikers Island, where he would spend the next six months awaiting his day in court.

In April of 1981, the case went to trial. Assistant District Attorney Edward Schoenman, the prosecutor, had previously offered Cliff a chance to plead guilty to manslaughter, with a possible two-to-six-year sentence, rather than murder, which could involve a life sentence—but Cliff refused, citing his absolute innocence. The Jones family had no money to hire an experienced defense attorney, but Cliff's sister-in-law convinced an elderly family friend to represent him in court. The man was a real estate lawyer with no significant trial experience, Cliff told me. "They bullied him." The trial transcript seems to indicate the court's attitude was closer to exasperated pity, however: at one point the judge called Cliff's defense lawyer up to the bench to explain a serious legal error he was about to make, which prompted the attorney to change course.

In the courtroom Schoenman laid out a table's worth of menacing evidence: the steak knife that killed Hernaiz, a used hypodermic needle, the blood-soaked hat the assailant was wearing, the victim's torn undergarments. Yet none of it had any physical link to Cliff—not fingerprints, not blood, not hair, not semen—nor did Schoenman ever attempt to connect any of it to Cliff, content to provide the jury with the window dressing of urban degeneracy.

The prosecution's case hinged on a sole eyewitness. Other people had witnessed the murder—Hernaiz's mother- and father-in-law—but no one else identified Cliff as the assailant. Midway through the trial, Schoenman informed the judge that a new witness had come forward, a person previously reluctant to go on record. Schoenman asked the judge to put the trial on hold until the new witness could observe Cliff in a lineup, acknowledging in a private sidebar with the judge and Cliff's defense lawyer that a single eyewitness did not make for a particularly persuasive case. Yet when the new witness failed to pick Cliff out of the lineup, Schoenman dropped the matter and this information never reached the jury.

Only Robinson would testify that Cliff was the perpetrator. The prosecution staked their case on the notion that Robinson was an especially good observer with ample time to get a clean look at her attacker. Yet her description of the perpetrator shifted and looped across the ten months that separated the incident and the trial. At the crime scene Robinson told police her assailant had an Afro. In the hospital, just a few hours later, she told Detective Holland the perp had braided hair. Later still, on the official police report, the perp once again had an Afro but was now described as stocky. In court Robinson was adamant her attacker had braided hair and was dark-skinned. Cliff is neither stocky (6'2" and 168 at the time of his arrest), nor did he have braided hair (an Afro during the period of the crime), nor was he "dark-skinned"—a point which Robinson, herself Black, conceded from the witness stand. Kenneth Jones, visibly distraught during Robinson's testimony, was removed from the courtroom as he muttered and objected to Robinson's vacillating description of her assailant, which seemed to match his brother only when the prosecution needed it to.

Perhaps most troubling was the nature of the live lineup where Robinson definitively identified Cliff. On the late October day when the Jones brothers went down to the precinct, Robinson was at central booking on a prostitution charge. She had been addicted to heroin for fourteen years and had, in 1980 dollars, a $50-a-day habit. In the previous two years, she had been arrested for prostitution more than twenty times, as well as for grand and petit larceny. When Detective Holland realized that Robinson was in custody, he had her transferred to the precinct to see if she would corroborate her earlier photobook ID. During Robinson's testimony in court, she mentioned that before she viewed Cliff in the live lineup at the precinct, Detective Holland had showed her some photographs—then immediately backtracked from this claim. It would be a shocking violation of protocol if true: Holland priming Robinson to remember whom she had selected in a heroin-impaired state from the photobook a month prior. It was an inconsistency that went unresolved, although it emerged that after Robinson cooperated with the live lineup, her most recent prostitution charges and fines were vacated.

With the People's case nearing its conclusion, Schoenman prepared a final piece of courtroom stagecraft. Robinson had said her assailant had a gap between his front teeth, as well as other chipped teeth. With the judge's approval, Schoenman compelled Cliff to stand before the jury box and bare his teeth so the jurors could examine them for chips and gaps. Then Schoenman ceded the floor. If his intention was to draw a direct comparison between a racist criminal justice system and the barbarities of American slave auctions, it was an apt closing image.

Cliff sat in silence throughout his trial. He was never given the opportunity to testify. His defense attorney, who was white, told the judge during sentencing that Cliff would "in terms of the way he speaks and expresses himself, not make the very best of witnesses." And so on April 15, 1981, the jury—white and Black and generally representative of the city's demographics—found Clifford Jones guilty of second-degree murder, first-degree rape, and first-degree attempted robbery. Kenneth Jones erupted in anguish from the gallery. The transcript preserves his interjection—*The fucking description!*—which he called out as the foreman read the verdict.

Three months after the jury found him guilty on all counts, Cliff appeared before the bench to receive a sentence of eighteen years to life. Here he was given his first and only opportunity to address the court in any substantive way. "I came forth when I heard the police were looking for me," Cliff said. "I thought I was being a law-abiding citizen for doing so, because I believe in the system." He looked at the judge. "I am innocent."

2.

One muggy autumn day I met up with Cliff at the Museum of Natural History. Manhattan was sunk in mist. He wanted to introduce me to a buddy of his, a basketball friend from the old neighborhood, who now worked as a senior photographer at the museum. In a staffroom down a dim corridor, Cliff and his buddy speculated whether anyone from the crew could still hoop. Was it that court on 105th or the one at Booker T. where Peanut dunked all over Roy and made him mad so many years ago? And whatever happened to Harvey and Bristol Cream and Ronnie Ride and Mervin? Cliff said one had made it to the NBA, briefly, or maybe it was the ABA. When reconstructing the distant past we sometimes settle for close enough. We strolled the dinosaur gallery, the titanosaur looming above us in a darkened hall, its bones lit the color of orange sherbet, its gracile tail slicing the air overhead. Cliff told me how he used to run through Central Park with his friends, off the city's grid and unsure how far south they'd come. When they reached the museum they would take refuge in its serene gloom. We lingered before vitrines polka-dotted with children's handprints, trying to envision the fossilized past.

Over the decades that followed his sentencing, Cliff was housed in ten different correctional facilities throughout the state of New York, from Gowanda, near Lake Erie, to Dannemora, up at the U.S.–Canada border. During this time, he said, he developed an array of techniques—temporal, psychological—that helped him navigate his years inside. Cliff's lexicon is still larded with jailhouse koans and strange slippery turns of phrase. "A year is taking your coat off and putting it back on," he told me once, referring to the cyclical actions he performed each spring and winter and spring as he headed to the exercise yard. He began to perceive time in swaths perhaps inaccessible to those outside the corrections system. "It may sound strange, but jail is not a university, where you think scholarly. If I've got to put five years in a box? That's two parole boards." He came to understand his lengthy sentence as a task to be completed—onerous, brutal, but something that could be achieved incrementally. Each morning Cliff got up and punched the carceral clock, and each night he punched out again. Across the years, he wrote letter after letter—to TV news stations, reporters, lawyers, law schools—hoping one day someone would listen.

He came to envision his solitude as a physical presence that could sit in the corner of his cell and keep him company. He read constantly, all the Harry Potter books, spy thrillers, espionage stories. "I did a lot of traveling," he told me. "At one point I could name twenty airports, and I ain't been to none of them." His general rule was to avoid interacting with anyone he hadn't seen on the cellblock for at least five years. New residents only provided opportunities for disorder, people desperate to establish status, men who snitched or stole or simply disappeared, released into freedom before a meaningful relationship might develop. Cliff's world became one of glancing, skin-deep encounters.

Eighteen years into his sentence, he appeared before the parole board for the first time—his first opportunity for release. "I'm not coming there with an attitude," Cliff told me, "just to talk some sense into them." When he proclaimed his innocence, as he had done unwaveringly since his arrest nearly two decades prior, the board waved him away, defective in his refusal to pantomime remorse. His release date drifted off into a murky and undefined future.

A terrible new temporal cycle began: parole board appearance, protestation of innocence, *Take two years and think about it*. The nauseating irony was not lost on Cliff that if he had pled guilty to manslaughter, or even feigned remorse, he would no longer be locked up. He watched people serve their sentences, get released, and then return to prison years later. These men would stare at Cliff, dumbfounded, ask if he had violated parole or committed another crime. *When are you going home?* "I couldn't give them an answer," he said. These encounters left him humiliated and powerless, sapped of standing in inmates' eyes. "You're an intelligent person, you're a grown-ass man—and you don't know when you're going home?" Prison provides little opportunity for ownership, but knowledge is one of the few things someone can lay claim to: how the system works, whom to trust, when the punishment will end. "When someone asked when I was going home," he said, "it fucked me up so bad I would just walk away." He began to sink into depressive states.

The years ground on. Cliff witnessed riots, murders, and all manner of interpersonal degradation. One season he watched the guards pick on a man in a wheelchair, harassed for weeks, until the man finally snapped and stabbed one of the guards with a handmade knife he'd concealed in his wheelchair for protection. Another time, in the aftermath of a riot that had been quelled, Cliff was among some inmates shunted into a processing pen. One of the guards told Cliff to lie on his stomach while the inmates were counted, but Cliff figured the guard would lay into him with the billy club once he complied. In defiance, he lay on his back: any act of violence would have to be administered while looking him in the eye. The guard stood over him and smirked, Cliff said, and as soon as he was counted and up in line, the guard clubbed him in the back of the head.

"You ever been around a thousand people where nobody knows you?" he asked me. "That's the feeling. You don't know nobody and nobody knows you." Prison was a strange anti-community, a photonegative of collective living. "You see these people 365 days of the year. Some come, some go, some you see get killed, some you see lose family members, you see their relationships fall apart. You see lots of misery—but there's no company. You're on an island."

3.

For two years I traveled to New York to hear Cliff's story. During these trips we mostly walked the city, taking wintry laps around Yankee Stadium, around Madison Square Garden. We marched the narrow canyons of the Garment District, past storefronts where spools of thread lay jumbled in piles like a bag of dumped jellybeans. Throughout our conversations Cliff was contemplative and proud, sometimes angry, although he always navigated toward more positive emotions. Cliff's instincts for gratitude and empathy were ever present. He told me in prison he felt compassion for the "real rapists and murderers," people from traumatized and violent lives, people who couldn't stand their own company. They'd been raised in environments in stark contrast to what he had known growing up.

His family sustained him. Cliff was originally one of four brothers. His oldest brother died from injuries incurred in a plane crash, in the 1970s, before he was locked up. His younger brother also died, of a blood disorder, after he had been inside for fifteen years; Cliff was allowed to attend the Harlem funeral in shackles, two guards loitering in the back of the room. But Cliff and his older brother Kenneth kept in close contact. Kenneth would visit and write letters, send books and magazines and money to Cliff's prison account. Eventually Kenneth moved to Georgia but still made regular trips to New York to see Peanut. Their mother went to great lengths as well: she worked in a school cafeteria in the Bronx and would head upstate at 5 a.m. on Saturdays, traveling via a chain of buses, trains, and correctional vans. When the weather prevented her from traveling, she sent food packages. Frequently she brought along grandchildren and other relatives, so Cliff would know he had the support of his extended family. In later years they were children who had never met him, born after he'd been locked up.

These visitors occasionally found Cliff anxious and depressed, but their presence buoyed him. "One visit could be good enough for six months," he told me. "You don't have to come see me every week. Just that one time, I can feast off that for a year." He saw his family as a force in opposition to the perpetual abrasion of prison life. Inmates would churn through their days, isolated and hateful, guards would stalk the cellblocks, fearful and disgusted, everyone mired in mutual distrust. "But I got love," Cliff said, "I got somebody that answers the phone."

This familial through line allowed Cliff to maintain his sense of identity. Prison is designed to disorient and deracinate, to snip the thread of self. By cutting you off from the community where you are known and understood, its goal is to make you illegible to yourself— you become then not a person but Inmate 81-A-3316, a manageable item to be filed in a cell. So when the anti-community of prison life began to erode his sense of identity, when he began to feel his fundamental Cliff-ness start to drift, his family would come to shore up the foundations.

Sitting in front of Madison Square Garden one afternoon, Cliff told me how he used to go time traveling in prison. Let's say it's Friday night on the cellblock. It's the start of the weekend—even in prison, somehow, this means something, those old rhythms of occupation and release sunk deep in the bones. Cliff would lie on his bed and travel back through his life, revisit a warm July night when he was playing basketball with his friends, could even walk back though the movements of a particular game, the way he'd finally blocked his big brother. Afterward they'd find a public pool, hop the fence and go swimming, pass some beers around, pass a joint around, drag deep, blissed on the sweet vibrations of the weed. He could feel that post-game looseness in his muscles, endorphin-flushed, the sensation of a body unclenching. What could be finer, drifting in the water with your real ones around you?

I told Cliff how painful it sounded to dwell in that fossilized world and he cut me off quick—*No, no, no*—brown eyes wide.

"Those memories saved me," he said. "That's how I made it."

4.

Cliff's jailhouse letters filtered out into the world over many years, primarily to silence and indifference. One of them, however, reached Adele Bernhard, a professor and attorney prominent in the world of wrongful convictions, who runs an innocence clinic at the Pace University law school. Bernhard struck up correspondence with Cliff and, in 2008, passed along his file to a lawyer named Kristen Santillo, who was a young associate at Cleary Gottlieb Steen & Hamilton, a global billion-dollar law firm. Santillo had taken the previous year to clerk and do volunteer legal work before returning to the firm. When she read Cliff's file, Santillo was intrigued. "I could see how weak the evidence was," she told me. She began digging into the archives—copying disintegrating transcripts from 1980, filing records requests with the District Attorney's office—and soon became obsessed with his case. "It was all based on one eyewitness identification," she said, "and the witness was so unreliable." After convincing her supervising partner the case had merit, she brought it to another young associate, Ryan Becker, and the pair took on Cliff's case pro bono.

I had known Becker years before, in college, and it was he who first told me about Cliff. One day he explained their legal strategy to me over the phone. "We knew from reviewing the records that there was physical evidence collected. And theoretically it could still be there. So if we could find the evidence—maybe, maybe, *maybe*—we could do some DNA testing." DNA fingerprinting had been invented during the years of Cliff's incarceration and by 2008 the technology was relatively commonplace in the legal world. But no one knew if the evidence from the trial still existed or whether it would be testable after thirty years.

The pair filed a 440 motion, which questioned the validity of the original conviction based on the likelihood of new evidence. "Back in 1980, people thought eyewitness testimony was the gold standard," Becker said. "We now know it is literally the least reliable form of evidence, because people's memories are so fallible." The last several decades' worth of neuroscience had shown that high-stress and traumatic situations impede memory encoding, formation, and retrieval, and so the D.A.'s case had become increasingly flimsy and irresponsible in the intervening years—this, at least, was Santillo and

Becker's argument. They just needed something to test. And to their satisfaction the judge agreed with them, compelling the D.A. and the NYPD to unearth the old case files and hunt up any relevant evidence. Unfortunately, the city reported, there was nothing left to test. All the physical evidence had been destroyed—the murderer's blood-soaked hat, the knife, the rape kit, the victim's clothes. The City of New York can't hold all evidence from all cases in perpetuity, and Cliff had exhausted his appeals back in the early 1980s. It was a significant setback, but Santillo and Becker were determined to find another way forward. In the meantime, they were wrangling over documents the D.A.'s office wouldn't surrender. "They basically have a policy where they just say no," Santillo said. "Wide swaths of documents were labeled privileged." Yet the judge again sided with Santillo and Becker and directed the city to unseal the remaining files.

It was in this way, in July of 2009, that the city grudgingly produced a box of files from the D.A.'s office—and there, stapled to the box, was a manila envelope containing a packet of eighteen hairs recovered from inside the murderer's hat. "It was one of those Matlock moments that you never actually have in the courtroom," Becker told me. Had the envelope been properly filed back in the early 1980s, and not subjected to a moment of clerical inattention, it would have been destroyed with the rest of the evidence.

Yet even with material to test, the process was knotty. The hairs were degraded after thirty years and could only produce mitochondrial DNA, which can't identify a specific person, although it can definitively exclude someone. But any hair tested is consumed in the process, so Santillo and Becker faced an insidious calculation: since each of the eighteen hairs was a singularly precious and non-renewable resource, how many should they test? How many would be enough to convince the judge? What would happen when the city contested the validity and asked for more testing? And even if they parceled the eighteen hairs exactly right, the testing process itself could introduce error—one sloughed flake of skin from the lab tech could compromise the sample. It was an impossibly thin margin for error.

They settled on three hairs. But before the testing could begin, there was a final uneasy discussion to have. At this point Santillo and Becker had only known Cliff for a few months. He seemed trustworthy, they thought, had never once wavered from his claims of total innocence. But, as Cliff himself told me one day, "Everybody says they're innocent." Becker recalled their awkward phone conversation. "I said, Cliff, we're going to do this hair testing. So if there's anything you need to tell me, now's the time. If one hair comes back as you, we're screwed." Cliff was adamant: "Whatever you find—test it. It's not going to be me."

By February of 2010, they had their results. Mitotyping Technologies, one of the top mitochondrial DNA labs in the country, reported it had assembled a consensus profile from the three hairs, meaning they all contained DNA from the same person. And that person was unequivocally not Cliff Jones.

"I exhaled," Cliff told me. He had known what the results *should* show, but his decades of dealing with the police and the courts and the prisons and the parole board had instilled in him a single resounding lesson: nothing is given, not even the most fundamental truths. "I'm thinking the system's rigged," he said. "It had all been wrong. So with the DNA, I didn't know what they would do—something underhanded, because that's all I had experienced." The lab report was his first moment of anything even resembling a course correction. "I think I shed a tear," he said.

With their moonshot DNA result in hand, Santillo and Becker petitioned the judge to vacate Cliff's 1981 conviction, or at least reopen the case for a jury trial with the new DNA evidence. By June of 2010 the legal winds seemed to be shifting in their favor. Cliff—who had made his biannual profession of innocence to the parole board six previous times—was released unexpectedly. Becker interpreted this as a sign the D.A.'s office was on the ropes. "New York State does not parole murderers," Becker told me. "I am convinced that someone talked to the parole board and said, *Cut this guy loose.*"

Cliff was so unprepared for the decision that for several days he didn't realize he had won his release: he had thrown what he assumed was a rejection letter into his prison locker to open later, he told me, to avoid spoiling his weekend. Late that Sunday night he slipped into the communal bathroom and sat down in a stall to sneak a cigarette and take in the bad news. Yet where the last page had for twelve years read "Parole Denied," Cliff saw the words "Open Date" and a two-week range indicating when he would be going home. "I go to the sink, turn on the cold water, sprinkle it on my face," he said. "I couldn't sleep no more."

On a sweltering late June day, a happy mob of extended family and friends, Santillo and Becker among them, swarmed Cliff as he stepped beyond the prison walls. He hugged his mother without oversight or interference for the first time in thirty years. But the celebratory mood would only last so long. In October the judge delivered his opinion: three hairs' worth of DNA was unconvincing; the charges would not be vacated; the case would not be retried. Cliff was free to walk the streets but he would do so as a rapist and murderer under the supervision of a parole officer.

Over the preceding two years, Santillo and Becker had grown close to Cliff. They'd traveled to different facilities around the state to visit him, spent hours on the phone with him. "We met Cliff when he had been in prison for twenty-seven or twenty-eight years," Santillo told me. "And he still had hope, he still had family connections, he still had a sense of humor. He is the most resilient and spirited person I've ever met." She told me how Cliff called her from prison one day, asking for her address; he'd read about a major earthquake in Haiti and wanted to send a $5 check to the relief effort, but wasn't sure if it would work from his prison account. "I couldn't believe the compassion he still had for other people," Santillo said. "It was a powerful motivator to keep working and get a good result for him."

They appealed the judge's decision. *People v. Jones* dragged into 2011, 2012, 2013, 2014. Cliff dutifully met with parole officers and abided strict curfews. He registered as a sex offender. He found female parole officers reserved a special disgust for men labeled as such. They would come by his apartment at odd hours, "lurking," as Cliff put it, trying to catch him in violations, or make him wait unusually long times at his appointments, or cancel without explanation. On Halloween he was forbidden from leaving his apartment.

At the appellate court Santillo and Becker were again denied, a disappointing but not entirely unexpected result. Post-conviction claims like Cliff's mostly fail, since appeals courts make it difficult to introduce new evidence. Yet while the court denied a new trial, the panel of judges split 3-2, with the dissenting opinion specifically commenting on the unreliable nature of the People's sole eyewitness. Testing the remaining hairs, the opinion added, would produce "extremely useful information for the court." This result offered a glimmer of hope for a shot at the New York Court of Appeals, the highest court in the state.

A final obstacle stood in their way—a legal precedent from 1975 known as Crimmins, which barred the Court of Appeals from reviewing lower courts' decisions where a motion to introduce new evidence had been summarily denied. It was a precedent that predated the invention of DNA fingerprinting, and one that had become particularly fraught where advances in technology might shed new genetic light onto an old crime.

By the time *People v. Jones* reached the state's highest court, in 2014, both Santillo and Becker had left Cleary Gottlieb. Santillo had her own practice in New York and Becker had moved to Philadelphia to join another firm. But both attorneys stayed involved to the end, working on briefs and advising their former colleagues, who would now see Cliff's case across the finish line. Santillo was at home preparing for the birth of her twins when her former colleague Heather Suchorsky argued the case before the Court of Appeals. But charging up to the state's highest judicial body and demanding it overturn a long-standing precedent is folly, and so Suchorsky picked away at a minute logical gap in the lower courts' behavior until Associate Justice Robert S. Smith finally interrupted her: "Aren't you going to a lot of trouble to avoid simply saying to us, *What if Crimmins didn't exist?*" Suchorsky paused for a moment. "I wouldn't fight with you that that's correct," she said.

The justices then began grilling the People's attorney, who had argued that the proceedings were moot due to Crimmins. "So we're wasting our time sitting here," Associate Judge Smith asked. "You're saying that if the courts below decide that we don't look at DNA because we think DNA is witchcraft, this court is powerless to review that?" Chief Justice Jonathan Lippman jumped into the fray. "You got a witness who admits to being on drugs at the time when she makes the identification," he said. "Why wouldn't you hold a hearing?"

Adele Bernhard, the professor who had passed along Cliff's file six years prior, called Santillo after the oral arguments concluded. "I think they're going to overrule Crimmins!"

A month later it came to pass: the Court of Appeals ruled unanimously in Cliff's favor, overturning forty years of precedent and allowing him a new evidentiary hearing. After the decision came down, all the remaining hairs from inside the murderer's hat were tested—all eighteen were from a person who was not Cliff Jones. And during the appeals process, the Office of the Medical Examiner had uncovered old fingernail clippings from Hernaiz, the murder victim, who had grappled with the assailant; the scrapings from under his fingernails also excluded Cliff. All this evidence would now be admissible in a new jury trial, shepherded by a powerful white-shoe law firm, and set against testimony from the D.A.'s lone eyewitness, who had died in the intervening years. Even still, the city bickered for two additional years before finally agreeing to vacate Cliff's conviction outright. "The

D.A. has a nice way of clenching they buttcheeks," was how Cliff put it to me.

It wasn't until November of 2016 that his exoneration was complete. Former inmate 81-A-3316 arrived in the courtroom a convicted murderer and rapist, and after the judge rapped his gavel he was just Peanut again. Santillo and Becker watched misty-eyed from the back of the courtroom. Then the trio slipped off for margaritas.

5.

One October I visited Cliff at his new apartment in Midtown, a modest space with a stunning terrace sixteen floors up, the panorama spanning from the Hudson River to the Empire State Building. After several years, his wrongful conviction settlement with the city had finally come through. Cliff's first act was to buy his mother a house in Georgia, his next to find a comfortable place for himself. With the guidance of financial advisors he set up trusts for his nieces and other family members and paid out gifts to friends who had never abandoned him across the decades. As Thanksgiving approached Cliff was planning to fly the extended family down to Georgia for a reunion. In a few months, COVID-19 would burn through the country, preying especially on those residing in prisons and jails.

On the terrace Cliff dragged on a Parliament in the warm autumn breeze, kitted out in a shock-white Raiders jacket and matching flat brim. The following week would mark thirty-nine years since he and Kenneth had walked through the doors of the 24th Precinct. As we talked, Cliff's neighbor from the adjoining apartment came onto the terrace, which was divided in half by a long planter. When Cliff identified himself as the apartment's new tenant and me as a writer, the neighbor grew intrigued and Cliff withdrew. "He's telling my story" was all Cliff would say. As we stepped back into the apartment, he had a tiny smile on his face. "Now he's wondering who the fuck I am."

The apartment was decked out with sports memorabilia, lanyards from VIP sporting events, and a framed photograph of Cliff and Kenneth at that year's Super Bowl. They'd gotten to work reclaiming lost days. Around the room hung pictures celebrating Black excellence: famous civil rights leaders, scientists and inventors, the bankers of Black Wall Street. Cliff caught me eying a reproduction of *Negro Boys on Easter Morning*, Russell Lee's famous 1941 photograph, where five kids in suits and ties lean against a Pontiac Silver Streak, staring defiantly at the viewer. "I look at that and think about my friends," Cliff said. He'd been chewing on a toothpick as we sat in his apartment, and by this point he'd reduced it to splinters. "Many of them are gone now."

He still struggled with an anger that could wash over him at unexpected moments. Money could not compensate a stolen life. "I couldn't mourn with my family when my little brother passed away," he said, "when my grandmother passed." He spoke of anxiety and depression, stewed over decades of mundane grace he'd been denied— his mother's face at the breakfast table, the smell of coffee permeating the old apartment. "Instead you in the mess hall with four hundred hungry men." Perhaps most distressing was his sense that the role of fatherhood had been robbed from him, a topic that tended to unearth deep wells of sadness.

But Cliff's fundamental temperament is one of forward motion. "Anger is energy," he said. "You can do something negative with that energy or you can do something positive." Since his exoneration he had been mentoring teens and done work with The Innocence Project. He had also gone back to school and at age sixty-four received his bachelor's degree from the John Jay College of Criminal Justice, an attempt to understand how the system had so catastrophically failed him. One sun-washed May morning, I traveled out to Flushing to see Cliff graduate. He strode across the stage at Arthur Ashe Stadium, arms wide like a returning gladiator, a look of unadulterated satisfaction on his face. On the lawn in front of the Queens Unisphere, Cliff and his family posed for pictures: the eighty-six-year-old Mrs. Jones was looking sharp in her church hat, Kenneth was sporting a polka-dot bowtie and white fedora, and Cliff was goofing, playing Atlas, standing so he appeared to hoist the iconic metal globe overhead.

In the last few years Cliff had also taken meetings with the District Attorneys in Queens and the Bronx to discuss wrongful convictions. The question he was eager to examine with city officials was how to build a firewall against injustices of the kind he experienced. When it comes to wrongful convictions, eyewitness misidentification is the single greatest factor, and will continue to be until there is policy reform in the way lineups are conducted. Police misconduct is another shameful component: a report from the D.A.'s Office in Brooklyn highlighted twenty-five wrongful convictions in that borough just between the years 2014 and 2019; the majority of those cases were due to police misconduct, which ranged from generating false evidence to coercing confessions. Twenty-four of the twenty-five exonerees were people of color. Prosecutor misconduct is an issue as well, present in more than a quarter of cases the National Registry of Exonerations has tracked since 1989. This is due in part to the system of advancement for prosecutors, which incentivizes them to chase win percentages and avoid surrender even in the face of mounting likelihood of innocence. Yet only one instance of prosecutorial misconduct—out of more than seven hundred recorded—has resulted in a prosecutor facing jailtime: Ken Anderson, who spent five days locked up after his deliberate obfuscations resulted in an innocent man serving twenty-five years in a Texas prison. Kristen Santillo told me several former colleagues who worked on *People v. Jones* have gone on to become U.S. Attorneys. "I'm glad they have the experience of knowing Cliff's case," she said, "for when they prosecute their own cases." Yet if the city can simply pay out the occasional settlement with no individual accountability, how likely is it to stanch these kinds of abuses?

While the human costs are unquantifiable, the financial costs are stark as well. A 2019 Yahoo Finance study found that U.S. taxpayers wasted four billion dollars over a thirty-year period incarcerating more than 2,500 people who were later exonerated. In the time since that report came out, several hundred more people have been exonerated. It will surprise no one who has remained awake into the year 2022 that this burden has fallen most heavily on Black men, who—despite accounting for 6% of the U.S. population—make up 50% of wrongful convictions.

That day on Cliff's terrace, he said he'd been thinking about his legacy. Going to prison for thirty years is a way of being erased, and Cliff was eager to make visible what had long been hidden. He said he had a vision of his story one day reaching some stranger in a doctor's waiting room. That person might tell his story to someone else, and someone else, and in this way his message—of persistence in the face of despair, of all the work that remains to be done—might radiate intimately into the world. He took pride in the fact that his decades of wrongful incarceration resulted in a new legal standard that would do tangible good for people in similar straits. His suffering might one day be sublimated into relief for someone he would never meet. "He opened the door for others," Santillo told me. "*People v. Jones*—that's his legacy."

But legacy is always hard to see in the moment. The picture clarified some months later, when, in April of 2020, to the great delight of Cliff and his extended family, he became a father for the first time, just shy of his sixty-sixth birthday. One afternoon in late 2020, Cliff texted me a picture of a gorgeously pudgy baby boy, smiling and swimsuited and splashing in a pool with his dad.

That was still to come, though. We left his apartment that afternoon and headed for street level, both of us with business elsewhere in the city. At the corner, Cliff hugged me and shook my hand. "I was fortunate," he said. "I was able to come home. But there are others. So how can you just find closure for yourself?" Then I watched his shock-white Raiders jacket bob down Ninth Avenue, weaving through the flow of pedestrians and into the bracing day.

BALLAD OF THE CURTAIN JERKER

I chugged a beer in the synagogue parking lot. Inside the wrestlers were slapping each other on the pecs, gassing themselves up, doing last-minute high kicks and headbutts and various kinds of erotic limbering. This is what I assumed at least, since I had not yet been granted a journalistic peek behind the curtain, literal nor metaphorical, to observe the wrestlers in their pre-show ministrations. *Patience*, I said to no one, then stomped my beer can flat and hid it in a planter beside the synagogue, to retrieve later and dispose of properly. *Take only photographs, leave only footprints*, just like in the Patagonia mailers.

This was in the deadheart of a Minnesota February, snow coming sideways off the Mississippi and sifting through the synagogue's custardy sodium vapor lights. Out along the river the trees were powdered sugar, the houses gingerbread, the whole scene quaint as fuck. I was on the Saint Paul side looking across at Minneapolis. Down below were those venerable sandy banks where, come summertime, the youth would smoke rollies around the greasy embers of burned pizza boxes, drinking Hamm's and hollering at campfires on the other shore. In the June dark, those fires offer up impossible branching timelines where the lovers are less gangly and groping, the hours less encumbered by Culver's shifts and summer school trig. One more twig for the blaze and would there were a raft to float across the broad back of the river and elsewhere.

But enough of this beery sentimentality: inside the Temple of Aaron, the squared circle awaits, eighteen feet by eighteen feet, with padded turnbuckles and slingshot ring ropes, the whole rig assembled just hours prior in the cavernous space that normally hosts Purim Carnival or Kosherfest. On the other side of the curtain, the wrestlers are doing final hammy stretches, adjusting Speedo bulges, bouncing in place as they envision the timing of an aerial corkscrew off the top rope. And there in the dark is Devon Monroe, #BlackSEXcellence himself, shaking loose his shoulders, about to twerk his way into our lives. I can hear the bell, let's go.

CHICAGO, NW SIDE

Okay, but first:

The last time I paid attention to professional wrestling was circa 1990, when I went to Mike Murphy's tenth birthday party to watch WrestleMania VI, available exclusively on Pay-Per-View. We smashed through the Murphy basement rec room, a sunken place filled with boxes of unlabeled VHS tapes and unpaired shin guards, and watched The Ultimate Warrior defeat Hulk Hogan, a result that split the room. Most of the boys were there in support of The Hulkster, understood to be the shirt-ripping paragon of American masculinity, although no one in the room had yet descended a testicle, so judgments into the nature of gender performance were potentially underinformed. The contrarians in the basement were pleased with The Ultimate Warrior's victory, but then Kev Dennehy said wresting was fake anyway, which we all more or less knew, but which sounded distinctly like sour grapes in the moment, so the birthday boy socked Kev in the stomach. That conflict was overshadowed when Zukowski dared himself to drink a Styrofoam cupful of all the different pops blended together, a "suicide" in our regional parlance, and straightaway vomited. The Murphy matriarch evicted us then into the night to run off our collective sugar high.

In early high school, I knew one kid who was very into professional wrestling, a small boy who delighted in feeding live mice to his pet snake. I watched him plop one of the squirming creatures into his terrarium some lazy Saturday afternoon: the mouse froze before the dead-eyed reptile, coiled in glacial stillness, and then the mouse was gone—a flicker of movement, a foot kicking frantically between the snake's jaws. That boy's room was plastered with wrestling posters. The Undertaker watched over this execution with us, his gaze steely beneath layers of goth eyeshadow and the lank inky veil of his hair. His pecs were agleam with oil, maple-glazed and set for the roaster. I felt a kind of sleepy nausea seep into my belly, began to sweat. I told the small boy I had to go and never came back.

American Legion #435, Minneapolis

One night my buddy Victor called me up.

"You want to come see the wrestling?" he said. "It's at the American Legion."

"Of course I want to come see the wrestling at the American Legion," I said, choking with indignation. I had not thought about professional wrestling for several decades at this point.

Come Friday night, the two of us stormed into the Legion, hot for combat. We swept past the horseshoe bar and into the packed community hall, the crowd adorned in flannel, camo, blaze orange, plaid, and Carhartt, all the shades of Minnesota's rainbow. At the inner bar, a woman jounced her infant in a Baby Bjorn as she waited on a Captain & Diet. High above us, the Preamble to the Constitution of the American Legion was painted across the walls, urging us toward *law and order*, enjoining us to *perpetuate one hundred percent Americanism*, to make *right the master of might*. When the National Anthem struck up over the sound system, so flag-bedecked was the hall that people were facing all different directions, hand on heart, each to his own personal Stars & Stripes.

Then the bell rang and some long-dormant instinct asserted dominion over my body. I blacked out briefly and came to screaming "Do your job, ref!" through mouthfuls of commissary hotdog. Ancient muscle memory had emerged violently intact. I watched an arrogant man in jodhpurs and turtleneck stalk around the ring, flicking his riding crop, and I booed the man in jodhpurs, my body shook as I cursed him. He wore a seedy blonde moustache, and while he did not physically touch it, his performance was that of a villainous moustache-twirl brought to life. Later, a cat-man in luchador mask entered the ring to a meowing claws-out chant led by the crowd. A gladiator in leather loincloth and shin greaves appeared. A man with green hair and green lightning bolt tights. These ruffians battled for our delectation, for our fealty. Between matches, wrestlers would address the crowd; we witnessed relationships crumble in real time (*once his bodyguard—now his rival!*), watched enmity blossom and alliances form. We roared in fury at the referee, that bumbling fool, who never witnessed the cheap shot, never made the three-count fast enough. We clawed our skulls in frustration as yet another pin was escaped: *One! Two! Thr—* "Two!" the ref would yell, wide-eyed, displaying two fingers for us as if holding the results of a stopwatch. "Only two!"

Some months later, I found a recording of this event online, the telecast from Channel 45. There, amidst ads for auto body shops ("Next to the Perkins!") and cutaways to the spokesman for the Hair Trigger Gun Shop (whose logo was a legally questionable repurposing of Yosemite Sam), I found unimpeachable evidence that I had not dreamed this beautiful dream. Directly in the camera's line, Victor and I cackle like lunatics, calling for blood. Something inside me had thawed, the thirty-year winter that clutched my heart losing purchase.

Temple of Aaron, Ringside

During the many years in which I had not thought about professional wrestling, one of the questions I had not thought to ask myself was: "Where do wrestlers come from?" Did they not emerge from the void, juiced and jacked and frothing for turnbuckle-launch? It had not occurred to me, in the time I had not thought to think about wrestling, that there might be an indie circuit, a farm system.

So it was that I had come to the Temple of Aaron that snowy February night, to see an event put on by a Minnesota indie promotion called F1RST Wrestling. I did not question the religious nature of the venue; as a youth, I had attended enough ska shows in suburban church basements to know that all you needed was space and some folding chairs and you could get your wig blown right out.

The synagogue crowd was different from that in the American Legion, more skater punk than hunter chic. I surveyed a room of well-loved hoodies with iron-on patches, low checkerboard Vans, black T-shirts covered in thin spidery script, hair that skewed pastel and neon and dyed-black. Through the room wafted undercurrents of Christian metal. The camo-baseball-cap contingent was present in smaller numbers, as well as two women in their sixties, who sat off by themselves hooting vigorously for their favorite wrestlers. In the front row was an outing from a group home, and a few rows behind them a father wrangled his five-year-old daughter, who was wearing a pirate hat and jumping on her chair. People were spaced widely through the airy hall and masked against COVID-19.

Out from behind the curtain came The Carver of Cutter's Alley, some monster movie figure, a knock-off Leatherface wearing a patchwork mask of human skin. He shuffled around the ring, bellowing at the crowd, fingers clutching and grasping involuntarily. The Carver's opponent was Rylie Jackson, a bleach-blond pretty boy just endearing enough in his arrogant gym rat bit to draw most of the crowd's support. He was sporting a doctored T-shirt—sleeves lopped off to display his bulging arms, midsection chopped to present his chiseled abs—and bright gold tights with the slogan CREAM OF THE CROP TOP plastered across his fundament. For ten minutes the beautiful loudmouth endured strangulation and turnbuckle smashing, flopped around on the mat like a dying salmon, an empty vessel into which The Carver poured his boundless savagery. Rylie Jackson was certainly concussed—we could nearly see the Tweety Birds circling him—but then he recovered miraculously, folded The Carver into a pretzel hold, and got the tidy three-count. He skipped off to mug for the crowd. While The Carver of Cutter's Alley had the integrity to accept his defeat, the inhuman beast brought forth a car tire he'd hidden under the ring and smashed the showboating Jackson unconscious before zipping his victim into a body bag, all to the referee's grave and bootless disapproval.

A diverse array of physiques passed through the ring that night, from beer bellies to muscular linebackers to compact gymnast bods. Male wrestlers and female wrestlers, meaty lads with ham hock arms and scruffy hipsters with muffin tops pouching over their briefs. The youngest combatant was a sixteen-year-old woman—the fan favorite Billie Starkz, The Space Jesus, who hails from beyond the stars and also from the greater Louisville metro area. She had arrived earlier that day with her stepfather. Tonight she would hoist her opponent upside down and piledrive the woman's skull into the mat; tomorrow she would return home and finish her Brit Lit essay before sixth period. Through a slit in the backstage curtain, I could see wrestlers who had been locked in mortal encounter just moments before now bro-hugging and doing a quick postmortem on their set.

The night's most captivating match involved a four-man battle for the championship—and into the arena breezed Devon Monroe, a young Black man, overtly queer-coded, with the graceful muscular body of a ballet dancer. Monroe was all trim lines and angularity, leapt over the ropes and began to twerk in his pink undies and fishnet tights. He blessed the crowd with a flashbulb smile, slapped his ass, and strutted to the corner to await his opponents.

Monroe was followed by The Anarchist Arik Cannon, the current champion, a sturdy gentleman who bore the general dimensions of a beer keg. Cannon's hair was long, his beard a bushy red, his red plaid tights decorated with the anarchist symbol. These two men seemed cartoon opposites, destined to clash—Monroe's style was athletic and nimble, Cannon's brute decisive violence—and indeed this came to pass when they eliminated the other two wrestlers. The duo squared off to the crowd's delight and launched into an elegant brawl of leapfrogging and chest-chopping. The five-year-old pirate a few rows up dervished around her seat, trying to mimic Devon Monroe's bouncy repertoire, until she upended her chair and went ass over teakettle onto the floor. The tiny buccaneer took one stunned moment there and then popped up to continue her calisthenic display.

The stew thickened!—The Anarchist Arik Cannon was not only an old-guard brawler but was in fact Devon Monroe's *mentor*, had trained Monroe at a local wrestling gym. We were witnessing teacher v. student, straight v. queer, white v. Black, old school v. new—an entire charcuterie board of potential Twitter discourse. The Anarchist had Monroe twisted into a painful hold, bent him into knots, he was in agony, but the audience began slowclapping Monroe back to life and suddenly he broke free. Cannon goggled in disbelief.

Devon Monroe, in the end, could not match Cannon in beef nor viciousness, was brought low by a Tornado DDT into a Twisting Neck Breaker, such was the announcer's autopsy. But as Monroe lay exhausted on the mat, Cannon summoned the mic. He would offer Monroe a rematch—one on one, no other wrestlers, no interference—

for the title belt. The fight would take place at this same venue in a few weeks, and the tickets were *on sale now*. Devon Monroe rose with great stoicism and shook The Anarchist's hand, defeated not broken. I couldn't buy my ticket fast enough.

In the parking lot, the snow was dying down. I saw the two older ladies call out to another family, a mother and father with their late-teen daughter. From a polite distance I eavesdropped. They all seemed to know each other from the indie wrestling scene. "I think we met you down in Iowa last year," I heard the older ladies say. The group bemoaned COVID-19, how it had disrupted their communities, how they were hoping to get vaccinated as soon as possible. But they were delighted to be back, the parents said, maybe the first signs of life reopening.

"See you at the next one!" the older ladies called out, heading for their car.

United States of America (19th c. to Present)

That night I went home to read up.

Somehow, across the decades and without my personal attention, the world of professional wrestling had endured. The enterprise emerged from the traveling carnivals that toured the country in the back half of the 1800s—P.T. Barnum stuff, Huck Finn stuff—populated with strongmen and bunco artists who barnstormed town to town, hustling the local rubes who thought they were gambling on genuine matches. The early world of professional wrestling was an insular one of codewords and carny slang, the most famous of which—*kayfabe*—stood for the craft's straight-faced refusal to acknowledge that its outcomes were predetermined, its characters' biographies fabricated.

A wrestler named Lou Thesz detailed this world in his autobiography, *Hooker*. (A "hooker," in grappler's argot, was a term of high art—a virtuoso on the mat who also knew the dark art of carny tricks and painful illegal holds.) Thesz began wrestling in the early 1930s and carried down lore from the previous generations; he claims authentic matches were almost unheard of when he started out. Thesz eventually became a superstar during pro wrestling's first golden age, in the 1940s and '50s, which ran parallel to the rise of television. During this period, kayfabe was strictly observed: no one broke character, no one copped to the scripted nature of the entertainment.

Pro wrestling saw periods of feast and famine over the decades, but by the 1980s it had become a dominant pop cultural lodestone, producing entertainments both live-action and animated (*Hulk Hogan's Rock 'n' Wrestling*), or even culinary (cf. the wrestling-themed restaurant Pastamania!, which Hogan himself launched at Minnesota's Mall of America). This period gave rise to wrestlers so famous they might become movie stars, or, in the case of Jesse "The Body" Ventura, movie stars who might later govern the state of Minnesota. Unknown to me at the time was a 1989 political hearing wherein the World Wrestling Federation—home to Hulk Hogan and superstars like André the Giant—sent a lawyer to testify before the New Jersey State Athletic Commission, averring that professional wrestling was not a "bona fide athletic contest" but in fact "an activity in which participants struggle hand to hand primarily for the purpose of providing entertainment." The WWF had broken kayfabe, on the record, to avoid regulation and to secure a tax break, those most patriotic of American legal endeavors.

Perhaps an aftershock from this notorious industry moment, the 1990s and 2000s were marked by a period of sweaty overcompensation which insisted that wrestling was not only real but *fucking intense, bro*. This was an era of 'roid-raging dudes in tiny swim trunks battering their opponents with barbwire-wrapped baseball bats. Women with fake tits flashed the audience and men with fake tits smashed each other with folding chairs, all of it set to a rippin' nu-metal soundtrack.

Contemporary professional wrestling seems to have pivoted

somewhat from the amped-up sexuality and baroque violence of preceding years. A hot new promotion, All Elite Wrestling (AEW), which airs its shows on primetime national cable, has tapped into the vibe of the indie wrestling scene, fusing Looney Tunes anarchy with wild athleticism and a healthy dose of internet-age self-awareness. One of AEW's stars, Orange Cassidy, is an undersized and marvelously agile tumbler whose shtick is that he doesn't care about wrestling. Cassidy—who came up through the same indie circuit as the wrestlers at the Temple of Aaron, before getting called to the big leagues—wrestles in blue jeans and aviator sunglasses, shirtless, hands planted in his front pockets, can't be bothered to remove them. I watched him in an AEW match where, for narrative reasons beyond my paygrade, Orange Cassidy wrestled the very serious Chris Jericho in a ring surrounded by large vats of "mimosas," which may or may not have been water and neon orange food dye. The winner would need to either pin his opponent or submerge him. Round and round they went on national television, each wrestler nearly winning by pinfall several times ("Two!" the ref shouted, forever showing two fingers to the crowd). But if the law of Chekov's Mimosa Tub teaches us anything, it's that by the third act someone's getting dunked in that motherfucker.

Do I need to tell you the indie slacker won?

Monroe v. Cannon (Round Two)

In April I returned to the synagogue to see whether Devon Monroe could steal the title from The Anarchist Arik Cannon. I was intrigued by what F1RST Wrestling was concocting, narrative-wise, pairing a queer Black kid with its stalwart old-school bruiser. It is perhaps not a stunning observation to note that professional wrestling has a long and troubled relationship with race and sexuality: this entertainment that traditionally saw Black men playing "pimps" or "thugs" or "African witch doctors"; this performance that long fueled its testosterone engine on gay panic jokes and generalized homophobia. Yet here came Devon Monroe, twirling his way into the ring, full hero's entrance, a tulle rainbow-patterned train flowing in his wake.

"From downtown Minneapolis," growled the ring announcer, "weighing 160 pounds, this is Black Sexcellence—Devon Monroe!"

Monroe, who is twenty-two, had been wrestling for less than three years. In 2018 he enrolled in the Academy School of Professional Wrestling, a training gym in Minneapolis run by a former WWE star. There he spent his evenings doing endless squats, practicing aerial maneuvers, and workshopping his in-ring persona. He loved thinking about the ways *person* influenced *performance*—how the strengths and limitations of his body might influence his character. Monroe had taken dance in high school instead of organized sports, but he'd been obsessed with wrestling since he was little, he told me, had an older cousin with all the action figures, all the video games, spent hours working through imaginary matches. "But I never saw any Black queer wrestlers on TV growing up," he said. He was eager to change that, and found a welcoming home at F1RST Wrestling.

And now here he was, center ring, young and hungry, ready to take down the champ. Monroe gave a flirty hip shake in Cannon's direction, his bellybutton stud glinting in the light. Cannon hardened his gaze, that glowering brute, and returned the hip shake.

Then they were upon each other. Cannon wrapped up Monroe from behind, but Monroe twerked his way out of the hold to the crowd's delight. The pair cha-cha'd through a polished combination of moves and countermoves, until Monroe launched the lean missile of his body off the ropes and slammed Cannon to the mat with an arm drag, the first big fall of the contest. Cannon responded by hurling Monroe out of the ring entirely and into the metal guardrail, pursued him with ursine relentlessness, delivering one openhand chop after another, the smack of meat on meat carrying up to the ceilings. Monroe was reeling, but again the crowd began to slowclap for him, and so he composed himself and smashed Cannon's head against the ring apron. Back inside the ropes Monroe found his angle. He sprung from the top rope, leveled The Anarchist with a flying jawbreaker, swept him into a pin—*One! Two! Three!* the crowd chanted—and we had a new champion, a stunning upset.

Here's the thing, though—and stop me if you've heard this one before:

In their final flurry of attacks and counters, and unbeknownst to them, Monroe and Cannon had smashed into the ref, boob eternal, who went down like someone flipped a light switch. We'd all witnessed it—an unambiguous victory for Devon Monroe—but with no ref to certify the pin, the match hung in limbo. Monroe looked around, still holding Cannon tight, searching for administrative validation, until from backstage a substitute ref came charging. The ref slid under the bottom rope with great panache, pounded out *One! Two! Thr*— but stopped short, hand hovering over the mat, and again we hung suspended.

With theatrical flourish the substitute ref tore off his COVID-friendly surgical mask and hopped to his feet: no ref at all, but the villain Darin Corbin—red-haired sonofabitch and blue-ribbon shit-stirrer! (At this time, I should note, I had never heard of Darin Corbin, but a scrum of highly caffeinated fans was happy to educate me on the indie scene's resident chaos agent.)

Devon Monroe gasped, the ring announcer gasped, we all gasped— and before Black Sexcellence could properly defend himself, Darin Corbin sprinted toward Monroe and landed his signature "Ginger Snap," a kind of flying headlock, which sent Monroe sprawling. The Anarchist Arik Cannon was woozily on his feet now but immediately met the same fate as Monroe. Darin Corbin stripped off his referee camouflage, stripped off his undershirt, and began strutting around the ring, bare-chested. He grabbed the mic and began to rant but before his screed could really gain any momentum, a tall man in a frog mask jumped into the ring—resplendent in green and yellow tights, holding aloft an oversized foam hammer of Thor—and Corbin blanched and fled backstage, fearing retribution from some act of skullduggery that predated my immersion in the timeline.

So that was that: no ref and no decision, just two wrestlers wandering groggily from the ring, the fiend Darin Corbin afoot yet momentarily neutralized, a classic instance of *deus ex machina* via Atomic Super Thunderfrog—just like Aristotle drew it up.

BALI, INDONESIA

In 1958, the American anthropologist Clifford Geertz and his wife went to live in a small Balinese village to study the local culture. During his time there Geertz came to believe that cockfighting, a celebrated local pastime, illuminated crucial aspects of Balinese culture. In his famous essay "Deep Play: Notes on the Balinese Cockfight," Geertz argues that forms of public play "can be treated as texts, as imaginative works built out of social materials." Entertainment has much to teach about culture, and for the Balinese, Geertz says, cockfighting is "a story they tell themselves about themselves."

For months now I've been on my own ethnographic journey, probing into what professional wrestling is and what it means, attempting to decipher the story it tells us about ourselves. The entertainments I encountered in the synagogue were unlike anything I'd seen before, some hypnotic fusion of Olympic gymnastics and improv comedy as read through the worldview of the Insane Clown Posse. I'd witnessed a kind of sports-based storytelling that united vaudeville, burlesque, and the plucky spirit of Triple-A Baseball. Particularly in the indie world, wrestling seemed to have reinvested in its roots, minus the stony-eyed insistence on "truth": it was a circus demimonde of body builders and clowns, daredevil acrobats and sleight-of-hand artists.

One afternoon I sat down in a wood-paneled Saint Paul bar with John Maddening, F1RST Wrestling's ring announcer, who had come to the group after a stint as the announcer for Minnesota Roller Derby, where his wife skated. (As Newton's Fourth Law of Motion states, indie wrestlers and roller punks must over time be drawn into the same orbit.) With his dyed-blue hair and electric blue business suit, Maddening serves as a delightfully hammy Master of Ceremonies, introducing the performers, egging on the crowd, and occasionally taking abuse from that evening's villains. One night I saw him rendered suddenly bashful in the ring, on the receiving end of a raucous and atonal "Happy Birthday" serenade from the crowd. When I asked Maddening what in the hell pro wrestling was anyway, he answered proudly and without hesitation: "It's a live-action stunt show with a soap opera element."

I tried to think of an analogous situation, where a sport with fixed rules and unscripted outcomes—Greco-Roman wrestling—had branched off into a parallel reality that involved the same general moves and physical postures, but also included the infamous 1998 "Hell in a Cell" match, wherein the fictional characters the Undertaker and Mankind fought each other atop a steel cage over a wrestling ring, until the Undertaker hurled Mankind twenty-two feet down to the floor, where he crashed through an announcing table and was hauled off on a stretcher, only to leap up with bloody mouth and dangling tooth to continue the match. I couldn't muster a good equivalent. Professional wrestling occupies a *sui generis* space in the culture, a strange nexus where *Star Wars*–quoting nerds and juiced-up gym rats might share space together and may in fact be the same person. It is one of the unique American artforms, like jazz, or comic books, or endowing corporations with the legal rights of people.

The French literary theorist Roland Barthes had some ideas about what was occurring in the wrestling ring. Barthes, who loved professional wrestling, included an essay in his 1957 book *Mythologies* called "The World of Wrestling." What appealed to him was a transparency rarely present in daily life, an earnest directness. "A man who is down is exaggeratedly so," Barthes writes, "and completely fills the eyes of the spectators with the intolerable spectacle of his powerlessness." Rather than hide his defeat, the vanquished wrestler "emphasizes and holds [it] like a pause in music." Wrestling provides "absolute clarity," Barthes argues, since "the function of the wrestler is not to win; it is to go exactly through the motions which are expected of him." When the hero wins, we delight in his heroic victory. When the villain wins, we delight equally in his achieving the perfection of form, the full flowering of his villain-ness. In this way, Barthes says, wrestling offers its audience "the perfect intelligibility of reality," lifting us above the "constitutive ambiguity of everyday situations."

Clifford Geertz writes something similar: "Like any art form— for that, finally, is what we are dealing with—the cockfight renders ordinary, everyday experience comprehensible...it catches up these themes—death, masculinity, rage, pride, loss, beneficence, chance" and orders them into "an encompassing structure." Both Geertz and Barthes saw dramatic play as an attempt to make our world coherent. When the bell rings, we might exist beyond the ambiguity that permeates our modern lives, we might witness clarity in a cloudy world—and if we're very lucky, we might watch a human being fly through the air and just once give the bastard his due.

MONROE V. CANNON (ROUND THREE)

On a blazing June evening, I returned to the synagogue for the rubber match, Monroe v. Cannon III. The mask mandate had been lifted in Minnesota and the crowd was bustling now, fans in wrestling merch milling around food trucks and hollering across the parking lot. The lifers were rocking their Zubaz pants—a piece of apparel created in the Twin Cities powerlifting scene and then adopted by the wrestling world and then 1990s sporting culture more broadly—the sartorial equivalent of perhaps-one-too-many psilocybin caps.

I ducked into the synagogue and caught a glimpse of Devon Monroe backstage in the sanctuary, pacing, dazzling in his silver lamé underpants and cape, backlit by a stained-glass window. Tonight was his night, I could feel it. First a close honorable loss and then an outright win stolen by the scourge Darin Corbin. I know how narrative structure works: part three is when the hero gets his.

Their match sparked off the night—Devon Monroe vs. The Anarchist Arik Cannon vs. Darin Corbin—a velocitized contest from the opening bell, title in the balance. Monroe showed off some acrobatic ropework early, but Darin Corbin parried his attacks and sent him flying out of the ring. Then Arik Cannon was down too, and the ginger villain covered him for the pin—what looked to be a speedy and shocking upset. But when Darin Corbin didn't get the three-count fast enough, and Arik Cannon kicked free, Corbin hopped up and got in the ref's face, petulant and carping. Something was off, though—it wasn't the usual ref but a large bearded dude I'd never seen in the ring before. After a beat I recognized him: none other than Rabbi Jeremy Fine, leader of the Temple of Aaron congregation and not-so-secret F1RST Wrestling superfan. Darin Corbin delivered a stiff two-handed shove to Rabbi Fine's chest—the crowd gasped, we loved gasping, were in perpetual gasp—but the Rabbi wasn't having it. He dodged the next attack and leveled Corbin with the bastard's own signature move, a fitting inversion of the previous show. Arik Cannon slid over and pinned the flattened Corbin to retain his title.

Devon Monroe limped valiantly backstage to cheering and applause—so close and once again unsatisfied. When you're twenty-two, the world is an endless two-and-a-half count, always on the cusp of that golden moment and forever denied. And the dumbass ref never sees it when you're great, and when you fail everyone's eyes are on you.

But no one stays twenty-two forever. "I feel like I'm still figuring myself out," Monroe told me one evening. He was talking about his in-ring persona, but the comment felt like it held broader resonance. "I'm still trying to figure out what Devon Monroe is." He was thoughtful and upbeat. "But that's just a part of the journey." He was still eager to win the title but trusted he would get another shot. For the current moment, though, he was concerned with things bigger than the game. "Representation is what got me into this," he said, "being an example for kids who might identify with me." He knew there were people in the crowd hungry to see someone like him succeeding at the highest levels.

Anyway, it seemed clear Monroe was bound for broader fame. In 2020, the industry magazine *Pro Wrestling Illustrated* listed him at #413 on their annual PWI 500, which ranks the five hundred best wrestlers on the planet. By 2021, he had climbed to #308—over one hundred spots in one year. He was booking gigs regularly, all around the country, balancing his day job against his hours in the gym, doing the extra reps, tweaking the details. Next week he was off to Iowa for Black Wrestlers Matter and after that were Pride and LGBTQ events throughout June and July, shows in New Jersey, in Florida. Things were getting busy. In his other life Devon was a bank teller, and it seemed inevitable that someday a guy cashing his paycheck would doubletake and laugh, recognize that red carpet smile—*Black Sexcellence, you rule, bro!*

As for The Anarchist Arik Cannon, that bearded bruiser? As it so happens, Cannon is the ringleader of this whole bizarro carnival, the creator of F1RST Wrestling. And at the risk of breaking kayfabe, when he's not the smashy anarchist pounding people on the mat he's a pretty friendly guy, enthusiastic and passionate about his craft, although you didn't hear that from me.

Cannon's been hustling his way through the wrestling world for twenty years now, chasing a dream that sprouted long ago at his grandmother's house. When they could see his parents' taillights in the driveway, grandma would flip on Verne Gagne's American Wrestling Association, Channel 9, and the pair would thrill to the wild showmanship and physicality of Minnesota's homegrown heroes. By the time he was a nineties skater punk, Cannon had tuned in to the outsider-defiant ethos that simmers below pro wrestling. He began training fanatically, ignored the people who said that at 5'7" he didn't have a wrestler's physique. Soon he was booking local gigs, bombarding regional promoters with demo tapes he'd filmed in his living room. By 2006 he'd managed to land a one-season role on the short-lived MTV cult classic *Wrestling Society X*. After a two-month wrestling tour in Japan, Cannon returned to Minneapolis and grew disenchanted with the local scene: too many lumbering bodybuilder types, too many shady promoters.

For a year Cannon had been sitting on a pot of MTV money and finally knew what he was meant to do. "We had all these talents who are smaller in stature but with the biggest hearts," he told me. "They're not being showcased." He would open his own shop, treat his crew fairly. At that time he was working security at First Avenue—the iconic Minneapolis rock club, home to Prince and *Purple Rain*—and he went to the management about filling some dead slots on the venue's calendar. So it came to be—F1RST Wrestling—home to the misfits, the performers who didn't necessarily have those 'roided-out wrestling bods (or sometimes did). It would be an organization that treated the audience not as rubes to be scammed but as an essential part of the performance. "Otherwise we're just assholes in costume beating each other up in an empty gym," Cannon said.

Whatever they were doing seemed to be working. F1RST shows were always sold out, and Cannon was constantly on the hunt for venues that would draw people who didn't consider themselves wrestling fans—breweries, street fairs—confident in the talent he could book, the spectacle he could engineer. With the help of Rabbi Fine they had survived a season of COVID homelessness; soon they would be returning to mega shows at First Avenue and other high-profile venues. F1RST wrestlers were starting to arrive in the national spotlight too: the brothers Darius and Dante Martin, two stunningly athletic high-flyers, recently signed a contract with AEW. Arik Cannon had landed some guest matches with AEW as well.

Maybe Devon Monroe would make it there too. With his physical ability, his charisma and fan appeal, his career smarts and industry supporters, it seemed within reach. But Devon knew that some people grind for twenty years and never make the leap. Maybe he would launch from those synagogue ropes straight off to Hollywood—like The Rock and John Cena before him—or maybe he'd work at the bank and wrestle on the side, or maybe he'd go to grad school, or maybe he'd get married and someday off in the future he and his husband would take their kids to the indie shows, get misty, say, *Dad used to be a star here*—maybe it would just be one of those beautiful passions that gives shape to the years.

For months I'd been thinking about *what* wrestling was, but it occurred to me recently the more relevant question was *who*. With its twerking queer men and no-bullshit women, its local beefcakes straight from the farm, its teens in Black Lives Matter shirts and buck-hunting bros, its dads and daughters and old ladies, the indie wrestling scene is one of the last places, maybe, where the punks and the good ol' boys can sit shoulder to shoulder and scream in unison *TWO COUNT REF ARE YOU FUCKING KIDDING ME*. So many people in the audience I talked with said they had become friends through indie wrestling, had gotten into relationships. One night I chatted with two buddies in their twenties, superfans who had met at a F1RST show. Kevin wore a Timberwolves jersey and a *Friday the 13th* baseball cap, used a wheelchair to assist a congenital disability of his legs, which could not bear weight; Dan was in an oversized Jacksonville Jaguars jersey and a Jags flatbrim, gave off a whiff of stoner-dirtbag affect, although I was perhaps unfairly primed by his outfit. One night some years back, Kevin and Dan realized they went to all the same concerts too—Kottonmouth Kings, Tech N9ne, ICP. Gesturing toward the wheelchair, Dan asked Kevin how he got to shows, and Kevin said he took the bus, or sometimes a few buses, but it was worth it. "Man, that's crazy," Jaguar Dan said. "I'll come pick you up!" Carpool buds for life.

We send our strange tendrils into the world, those curious passions and inexplicable pursuits to which we devote hours and years and decades. We let our unbeautiful fungal filaments creep through the damp and dark, and mostly we find nothing, and sometimes we find something—a tiny node of commonality, then another node, and eventually maybe a network. And one day someone gives us a ride to the show, and the world becomes a few degrees less lonely, a few degrees more legible.

Temple of Aaron Parking Lot, Minnesota

The wrestlers have packed up their merch, sold a few T-shirts, a few buttons maybe, and the crew has carried the ring piece by piece out to the U-Haul, laughing and talking shit, soaking in the tired buzzy satisfaction that comes at curtain fall. The fans are home deconstructing the matches on social media, or washing their new Darin Corbin shirt, and someone on the street will walk by one day and point at the shirt, smiling, shaking their head. The synagogue is empty now, lights clicked out, a massive silent bubble filling the space that was electric chaos an hour prior. The caravan is heading for the next show, the next town, taillights glowing in the vespertine June air. Down along the banks of the river the campfires are waking to life.

THE OPEN PITS

THE HIGHEST PUB ON THE AFRICAN CONTINENT is in the tiny enclave nation of Lesotho, up through the clouds. The establishment is closed to the public, inside a diamond mine, and not in the business of advertising its existence. Off beyond the pub are the diamond mine's two open pits, manmade canyons that span sixty acres. Along the haul roads that rim the pits, fifty-ton dump trucks crawl up from the earth laden with kimberlite ore.

From my vantage, the dump trucks looked like plastic yellow toys. I was standing outside the pub, chatting with my host, a high-ranking mining contractor, who would come to the diamond mine for three-week stints and then return to South Africa to see his family.

"We whites are struggling, you know," he said. The sun had begun to drop toward the mountains and the golden hour light was filtering across blasted terrain. He had been telling me how he wanted his son to attend the University of Cape Town, but was unsure if the boy would get in due to the racial quotas for the student body. "Before, when the whites were in charge, the Blacks were struggling," he said. "Now the Blacks are in charge and we whites are struggling."

A strange electricity rolled through my stomach. I wondered if I had misunderstood him, comparing his son's academic options to the brutalities of life in Apartheid-rule South Africa.

I had met this man only very recently. In a remote town in Lesotho, not far from the diamond mine, he had noticed my hat, which sported the logo of his favorite rugby side. We got to talking, and he invited me to come watch the team's big match on TV. I would be staying the night as a guest of the mine. The man seemed eager for company. I didn't tell him I had picked the hat from a bargain bin at the Bloemfontein airport because I liked its color.

The diamond mine spread around us like a moon base: corrugated metal outbuildings, a primary crushing unit, buttressed tracks that shunted earth and rock around the facility—all this apparatus 10,500 feet into Lesotho's highlands. In the approaching winter, the temperatures would drop well below zero degrees Fahrenheit. Beyond the walls of the mine, the roads were treacherous and impassable in the dark. We were miles away from anything.

My host and I headed inside the pub and joined a group of white managers who were sharing tales of the mining industry in southern Africa. A Scottish man claimed to be one of the first people working at this mine in Lesotho. "When I came here," he said, "there were four whites and three Blacks." He paused, a little smirk. "Someone had to pitch the tents." A different man began rhapsodizing about how Zambia had once been a wonderland, but had now fallen into post-colonial disrepair. "I can tell you why," the man said, although I hadn't asked, and he nodded significantly toward the far end of the bar, where the only two Black men in the pub were sitting. We were in the senior bar, where only management were allowed. The two Basotho men he nodded toward were supervisors one rank lower.

Another white contractor raised his eyebrows and began to speak about what took place in the Basotho laborers' dorms. "After dark they act like animals in there," he said, and my host just shook his head. "They don't appreciate anything, not the dorms, not the food, not the wages."

"Let's see what happens when we go," the contractor said. "This country would fall apart without us."

One of the two Basotho supervisors at the other end of the bar noticed I didn't have a stool and wordlessly brought his down to me. I knew how rude it would be to refuse his act of hospitality, so I thanked him ornately in Sesotho. I wanted to distinguish myself from the men in my party, but the words cracked hollow in my mouth.

When we finished our pints, my host wanted to show me the junior pub. The men led me to a doorway where we peered into the other side of the room, which was packed with Basotho laborers, men and women who laughed and drank and played snooker while famo music pumped from the speakers. "That's the dirty side," my host said. "You can wear your work coveralls in there, but not on this side." We returned to the stillness of the senior pub. Soon my host and I left to begin the braai. We were going to grill a feast for the rugby match.

My host must have sensed my discomfort. As we trekked through the crisp mountain air, he stressed how much he loved his Basotho employees. They were just in need of a little guidance now and then. When we reached his living quarters, my host's roommate was waiting, an older white South African engineer, ruddy-faced and silver-haired, pouring brandies in preparation for the match. They stayed in a large metal trailer up on supports, furnished with a few spartan bedrooms, a kitchen, a television.

The men had laid out a robust spread, far more than we could eat, even after the other managers returned from the pub: roasts and chops, coils of sausage, delicate shavings of dried biltong, a case of wine. "I love to cook," my host said and patted his round belly. "When I go back home, that's what I do with my wife—she chops the onions, I chop the tomatoes, we prepare the meat for the braai. It's our way to reconnect after I've been away."

"Me and my wife?" the roommate said. "We go to Ocean

Basket"—a South African analogue to Long John Silver's. This was his fourth wife, he told me later, thirty-five years younger than him, recently pregnant. "We sit there all night and share portions." He chuckled to himself. "But I can't eat the spicy pieces. Those are for her." He spoke with a clipped Afrikaner accent, as if someone had pulled tight the drawstring of his mouth. "That's our special time," he said. He was lost in momentary wistfulness, then rose to pour more brandies.

My host smacked him warmly on the back and they began to banter in father-and-son cadence. "We like to stay up talking," my host said. "We can drink a few beers together, I'll tell you that." The roommate laughed and shook his head. He went to fuss with the birdfeeder he had hung outside, chirping and whistling as he did so, his daily ritual to draw some graceful vitality to the abraded landscape.

Before I finish my story, I should tell you what came after.

This visit to the mine happened in 2015, during a six-month stay in Lesotho. After I returned to the U.S., I published my little narrative about the diamond mine in a magazine. I wanted to convey the racial dynamics I had witnessed, although I had no delusion of producing any tangible change. It was a gesture into the void. The telling of the story was complicated, too—there were vulnerable people involved whose identities I concealed and modified, details I shifted to protect the innocent. I was well aware of how the diamond mine could rewrite the livelihoods of Basotho people employed there. I decided not to use the names of the white managers, nor even the name of the diamond mine, which left me in a meek and compromised position. I wanted to shine a light without training the beam directly into the dim corner where it was needed—a kind of performative half-measure.

Anyway, it didn't matter. A month later a friend in Lesotho sent me an email. The diamond mine had encountered my article and had put out a press release denouncing what I'd written. They were indeed the unnamed diamond mine of the article, the release was eager to clarify, but they were certainly not a racist organization, since racism went against their institutional policies and bylaws. "It is therefore disappointing that Mr. McGrath did not make contact with the company," the statement continued, "and afford the mine the opportunity to emphasize that racism has no place here." The diamond mine wasn't angry with me, just disappointed. But the letter closed with a vague and to my eyes unsettling comment: the situation was being investigated further to see if action would be taken. The passive wording left it unclear whether this action would be directed toward me or toward someone else. I leaned back in my chair. I had never been sued for libel by an international mining conglomerate before. I wondered what the process entailed.

I received another message that was more direct. My host conveyed, through a mutual acquaintance, that if he ever saw me again he would kick the living shit out of me. His reaction was understandable—he had come to experience what Joan Didion had warned so long ago: "Writers are always selling somebody out." After all, had I not violated the fundamental sanctity of the guest-host relationship? I had been taken in, given shelter, lavished with food and drink, and then repaid them with contempt from across the sea. Ritualized hospitality is serious business in cultures around the globe and throughout recorded human history, from Ghana to Melanesia to the U.S. Pacific Northwest and beyond. In ancient Greece, the notion was called *xenia*. It plays a central role in *The Odyssey*: the bond between guest and host is sacred, and those who contravene it meet enthusiastically gruesome ends.

Throughout my evening at the diamond mine, I had been slipping into the trailer's tiny bathroom to take notes. I could hear the men just feet away, lost in happy raillery. I wanted to capture their phrasing just right, so I could sneer at them just right. I was entranced by their bare and utter humanness, could break my gaze only to scurry off and scribble in my notebook. I wanted to document all the ways these men were gentle and loving and seeped full of racial bile, intelligent and stunningly blind, isolated, lonely, their empathy cored out and replaced with an incurious blankness about those with whom they shared their days. My host's later threat of violence made perfect sense. Surely my circumstances atop the banal systems of racial brutality were closer to his than not. Wasn't my article just an opportunity to prove I was one of the good whites?

The rugby match was underway.

I ate and drank and reveled with those men, broke bread with them in that trailer in the diamond mine. We roared for our team, whose players' names I was still learning. Our side performed admirably, had taken a respectable lead by halftime. We poured brandies and slapped backs, bonhomie incarnate.

At the break my host and I stepped outside and warmed ourselves by the braai. It was full night now, the air crystalline and biting. It was time to cook the meat. As we talked, one of my host's employees approached in the darkness. He was a Mosotho man in a hard hat and reflective vest, a mid-level engineer of some kind, working the night shift. He had come to consult on a logistical question, some technical snarl at the facility that needed resolution. My host positioned the coils of boerewors over the flames, a meter's length of sausage, and the two men hashed out a solution to the problem.

The Mosotho engineer turned to leave, heading back for the primary crushing unit, which ran through the night. "Hey there," my host said, and took a swig of wine. "Pop down and grab me some wood from the hopper."

The Mosotho engineer looked confused. For a moment no one said anything. My host gestured then to the black void of the crawlspace beneath the trailer, a small gap where the supports lifted the trailer up from the dirt. The Mosotho engineer stared into the black crawlspace, then looked back to my host, smiling uncertainly. He was trying to decide if it was a joke.

"Go on, lad."

My host must have felt my gaze on him. He laughed uncomfortably, patted his ample stomach. "I'm too big to get down there anyway."

The Mosotho engineer looked again at the hole, made some silent calculation, then slid down into the dirt under the trailer.

I turned away. I stared off toward the open pits. Behind me I could hear the coil of sausage sputtering and popping on the grill and inside the other men toasting and cheering. After a moment the Mosotho man passed up a large armful of wood for the braai. He crawled out, dusted himself clean, and returned to the primary crushing unit to resume his operations.

My host took the meat off the braai. "We've got good boys around here," he said. "I'll send some airtime to his phone later, to show my gratitude." Then we headed inside to watch the second half.

The next morning, I gathered my belongings quickly while my host was at a meeting. As I packed up, a Mosotho woman came to clean the trailer. I greeted her in Sesotho and we talked for a bit before realizing we had a friend in common. In this stolen moment I asked what she thought of the diamond mine. "We work fourteen days and then go home for a week," the woman told me. "I don't want to be away from my children for that long, but I must have a job."

Later I would interview several Basotho former employees: no one liked the mine, but everyone accepted its inevitability. One woman described the place as a crucible of various tensions—between Black and white, men and women, urban people and rural—but she reserved a special tone of contempt for her fellow citizens. "There are Basotho who spy on other Basotho and report them to the managers, people who make themselves slave to the makhooa," she said, using the word for *white people*. Another former employee told me she hated the job— there were no grotesque abuses but plentiful small daily degradations. "Something there felt like Apartheid," she said. "But there are so few jobs. So you bow down to the manager or you get fired." The wages at the mine were well above average in impoverished rural Lesotho. Especially in the remote highlands, Basotho people were desperate for work, economic hostages pinned to the top of a mountain.

Later that morning I exchanged pleasantries with my host and left the diamond mine. I headed back across the road that was barely a road, the tundra climate in perpetual assault against anything resembling blacktop. My host and the other managers had sent me off with meat and wine, sweets for my children, even a new rugby jersey so I could cheer for the team and remember fondly our time together.

As I drove, a towering mound of pulverized waste rock loomed alongside the road, rubbly byproduct of the excavation process. It looked like the first peak in a curious new mountain range. Beyond it the diamond mine churned away, systematically grinding through slabs of earth until the glittery bits emerged.

STEEL TRACKS

1.

THE FIRST QUESTION TO CONSIDER is why he was fleeing.

The straightforward answer is that he was fleeing the Russian Army, and the more complicated answer is more complicated. There will be time for that.

2.

So: he was fleeing the Russian Army, the *he* of this story being Shia Bloch, seventeen years old, upstanding citizen of Shumilina District. As for the *when*—let's say 1905, although 1904 is possible. Shia came from a tiny nameless farmstead north of the Pripyat Marshes, in the Pale of Settlement, a skinny historical swath of eastern Europe that ran north-south through what is now Latvia, Lithuania, Belarus, Poland, Ukraine, and Moldova—verdant mucky terrain pocketed with woods and wetlands. It was the first place on the continent in three hundred years where Jews were permitted to own land. There in Shia's sleepy farmstead, dogs lay dazed in the sun and the houses were huddled like the hub of a wagon wheel, fields of rye and wheat spoking out around them. In that farmstead the available medicines were honey, beeswax, castor oil, and prayer; there were no telephones, no automobiles, no doctors, no jails.

At fourteen Shia left his farmstead for the town of Vitebsk, several days' journey on foot, where he would study Torah. This was a matter of some pride for Shia's father, to have a boy go off to rabbinical school, proof they were more than humble farmers. Although I wonder now if Shia's father would have sent him knowing what I know: that he'd never see the boy again. Or perhaps this was simply an understanding of that time and place, that any cleaving might be the final one.

The two years Shia spent at rabbinical school in Vitebsk (now part of Belarus) was the first time he had been away from home. Yet any pangs of longing for his family must have been tempered by Shia's realization that he was born for studying, his brain hot for all the arcane markings and symbols that differentiate us from the beasts. The one matter that did trouble him was food. At the rabbinical school, each boy was assigned a local family who would provide one meal per day, a practice called essen teg in Yiddish, *eating day*. The students were left to their wiles for any other meals, which meant there were none, and Shia spent those two years in a state of unrelenting hunger. Most of the boys didn't know the families they took their meals from, but Shia had first cousins who lived in the nearby hamlet of Shumilina, and so he was allowed to eat his daily meal with the family Nechamkin, although he was forbidden from living with these cousins. The rabbinical school was monastic in its vision, separation from family and sleeping on hard mats and food deprivation all being a kind of education. Or perhaps it was just the asceticism and isolation that accompany religious formation across many cultures, the better to bond young minds in spiritual fervor.

What must Shia have thought as he approached the Nechamkin house that first afternoon, the four-mile trek from the rabbinical school behind him? (There were no paved roads of course, and so the mud had sucked and nagged at Shia's shoes throughout the trudge.) He had never met his first cousins, this family of local merchants and entrepreneurs, and must have been stunned then to find his own dear mother inside preparing a meal of chicken and potatoes, his eyes blurring suddenly in the rich pungency of baking rye bread, which rolled in waves from the enormous brick oven that dominated one end of the kitchen. When he saw his mother, I wonder, did the giddy relief come in a flood or did it wash over him gradually, the way one wades by degree into the Pripyat River? And when his reverie dissipated and he realized this woman was not his mother, but his mother's identical twin sister, his aunt—the cockeyed smile not quite right, the timbre of her voice a shade too thick—did his stomach bottom out? Or was he too starved and too tired for this reversal to land with real weight?

And what of his cousin Sophie, two years younger than him, sharply dressed and such a talker. She was the youngest of ten, the family's pet, subject of her older sisters' cosseting—hair braided and doll-dressed and fussed upon endlessly. Did Shia notice her immediately? The house was roiling with older cousins and brothers' wives and so perhaps Sophie did not immediately swim into view. How greedily did he tear into the chicken that first night—there were fifteen at the table, and a lone bird, every scrap apportioned, the drippings from the pan drizzled across potatoes, gravy sopped with dark rye, every shred of flesh sucked clean before the smaller bones were molar-crunched. Was it then he noticed Sophie? Sated now and sleepy, belt uncinched, the heat from that great brick oven lapping gently at the family's cheeks—did he pick out Sophie's voice from the tempest of Russian and Yiddish, all the questions and stories and complaints and jokes layered over one another in familial cacophony? Did cousin Sophie cock an eyebrow at his patched and re-patched farm pants, his crumbling shoes? How immediately apparent were her charms?

Or did that come later, after they shared many meals, after they debated politics and argued matters of theology—*No, that's not what happens to the neshamah after death, it's not like that at all, dissipating into the air, and don't confuse neshamah with ruach either!*—their teenage brains aflame with lofty ideas. The hungers of that age are easily confused, and Shia's hunger was burning, endless—later in life he was a burly bull of a man—and so I can only imagine how his fourteen-year-old body sang out for calories, proteins, starches, anything fatty or savory, just one shovel of coal for the blaze. Romantic hunger calls out with the same unwavering bodily keening, so let us think of poor Shia, the way his mind and body throbbed—*sustenance, sustenance!*

Did they touch? I think we must assume so, for how in close quarters could they have avoided it, all those bodies jostling and tumbling over one another? Perhaps it was in the act of reaching for a heel of rye bread or shoving over a stool to make room. Even conversation could be a physical activity for the Nechamkin family—rooms stormed from in anger, forearms grabbed in impassioned plea—*Listen, I've seen trains full of soldiers heading for the front, it's no rumor, belting those patriotic songs as they go.* So yes, they touched, Shia and Sophie, an incidental brush of the fingertips perhaps, a hand rested in passing upon the shoulder.

For two years they shared meals in that house and for two years Shia and Sophie talked and bickered and laughed like best friends and respected rivals, like siblings, although they were cousins. And for two years Sophie's father grew increasingly cold and needling toward Shia; by the end, their spats would break across the dinner table the way storms are drawn out of marshland, the air ripe with moisture, then suddenly sheeting thickly around you. Sophie's father must have seen what was simmering under his roof—*insupportable, insupportable*—but before the matter could boil into outright accusation and embargo, word arrived that Shia's father had been killed in an accident back on the tiny nameless farmstead. (Rearing horse? Gangrenous plow gash? The record here is bare.) Shia left the rabbinical school then, left the family Nechamkin, found work in a general store, for he was now his family's breadwinner *in absentia.*

Out behind the general store Shia built a lean-to of scavenged wood and huddled in the evenings over a cookfire, frying onions and potatoes in a borrowed pan, then bedding down in hay to dream of Sophie. He lived that way for a year, a monkish life already well familiar, and sent all his money back to the farmstead. He visited the Nechamkin cousins when he could and wrote Sophie letters when he couldn't. And out in the silence of his lean-to Shia puzzled over the Talmudic riddle that was Sophie, attempting to parse the nature of their impossible relationship.

Then the Russian Army came for Shia Bloch and he packed a bag and fled.

(EMAIL FROM MIKE)

Nope—the last name was never spelled "Bloch." Ever. It was a four-letter Russian name ultimately rendered "Block" in the Roman alphabet. The great Russian symbolist poet of that period was Alexander Blok. People named Bloch are usually Jews of Alsatian or French origin.

(ON TABOO)

All cultures have an incest taboo, forbidding sex between people perceived to be too closely related. But this taboo is not inborn, for if incest horror were instinctual, it wouldn't need prohibition (just as we need no specific regulation against eating our own shit). True bodily revulsion doesn't require a statute to enforce it. The disgust one might associate with incest stems not from biology but from culture, and what is considered foul varies from place to place.

People across many cultures find the concept of sibling marriage repellent, for instance. Yet the historian Walter Scheidel tells us that brother-sister marriage was a regular occurrence in Roman Egypt, both for royalty and commoners. In the second century CE, census records for the city of Arsinoe, near the Gulf of Suez, note that 37% of documented marriages were brother-sister unions.

3.

Perhaps I've misrepresented this. The Russian Army didn't exactly come for Shia—*him?* farmboy rabbinical student?—although he did receive a draft notice to fight in the Russo-Japanese War, which is a way of saying he received a death sentence. At that time the Russian Army didn't issue guns to Jews, who were expected to provide their own weapon or scavenge one from a corpse or simply become cannon fodder—not a particularly vexing matter to the Russian Army.

But Shia would not die unarmed in a smoking muddy field in Manchuria. He was seventeen now and altogether too hungry for that, ablaze in the world, eating up the oxygen around him. He quit his job at the general store, packed a meager bag, and abandoned his lean-to. He wrote to his mother and brothers at the tiny nameless farmstead and explained that he was going. They would have to find a way without him. If he stayed he was dead anyway, and if he disappeared there might at least be hope. Then he paid a final visit to the family Nechamkin and blessed them for their years of kindness. Did he steal a private moment with Sophie, fifteen then, did he tell her he would write? Did Shia understand it was partly Sophie's impossibility that he was fleeing? There is no record of their parting.

Then Shia launched himself at the world. For three months he walked—but what was this after years of trudging daily between rabbinical school and Sophie's house, eight miles, ten miles? He was just as ravenous and just as penniless, although now it was the early fall and Shia was living outside, following the railway lines from Vitebsk to Kiev to Moscow, sleeping in the woods, dodging police and army, scrounging potatoes from fields and roasting them over small smoldering fires in the brush—a Belarussian bindlestiff adrift in the world. How immeasurable the land must have seemed to Shia then, forever walking, keeping those steel tracks in sight from the woods, sometimes in step with other draggletailed souls who whispered rumors of checkpoints ahead or snickered at jokes about little Vovochka, about the hare and the wolf. Often Shia was alone and softly humming, leaves crunching underfoot, emerging here to find a Jewish shtetl where he was given bread, emerging there to find a Cossack settlement where he was chased by men with farm implements. Throughout his sojourn the trees fired with color, the air bore the tang of seasonal decay, the days and nights grew steadily colder, September, October, November.

It was snowing in Moscow when he arrived. Shia was very tired and very hungry and so he went immediately to work in the stockyards. He knew how to handle cattle and soon found himself accompanying a cattle train to Saint Petersburg, feeding and changing the bedding of those somber steaming beasts. In Saint Petersburg he learned that men could smuggle themselves out of Russia on cattle freighters heading for England, and so he burned his identification papers and stowed aboard a ship bound through the Baltic Sea for Liverpool. He buried himself in hay that stunk of humid shit, a nest redolent of his agrarian childhood, and was discovered on the second day out of port. But it was too late to do anything with Shia other than cast him overboard or put him to work—and he was an expert and unflagging worker. In Liverpool he pulled this trick again, revealed himself once that ship was out to sea.

As he took up his labors on that freighter, he learned from his mates that the ship was aimed for Canada—that broad and open land where he would live out the remainder of his days.

(Malinowski, et al)

Here's another example: The third book of the Torah expressly forbids nephews from sleeping with their aunts—*You shall not uncover the nakedness of your father's sister*, Leviticus 18:12 warns—*she is your father's near kinswoman*. (Although it should be noted that Moses was, biblically speaking, the offspring of this exact kind of forbidden union.)

The Trobriand Islanders of Papua New Guinea, however, celebrate nephew-aunt sex—although only on the paternal side, for this is a matrilineal society. "Sexual intercourse with the father's own sister," Malinowski reports from the field, "is emphatically right and proper."

(email from Mike)

No one ever went to Moscow by way of Kiev in those days. That would be like going from New York to Chicago by way of St. Louis. And one did not sail for England or any point west by way of Moscow or Kiev, because neither inland city is in the right direction and neither was a Baltic port. The typical route would have been overland to Warsaw and then by rail to Hamburg.

4.

It is 1913 now. Over the last eight years, Shia, who is twenty-four, has made his way from Pier 2 in Halifax—typhus-tested and rechristened by a Canadian customs agent, Yeshayahu "Shia" Bloch/Blok/Block no more, now James "JB" Block heading west—all the way to Manitoba. Here the Canadian government is offering homesteaders free plots of Anishinaabe land.

Out past Prairie Grove, Shia cultivated 160 acres, dug a sod house from the earth, raised a barn, strung fences, irrigated, plowed, fertilized. The wind scythed across the terrain. In the summers he roasted on the plain and in the winters he huddled around a potbellied stove while his stomach boiled and his ass froze. It was a filthy life.

Across those eight years Shia sent money home to his family, and across those eight years Shia wrote diligently to cousin Sophie, who was now the sole proprietress of the Nechamkin family store back in Shumilina. Did they still discuss the finer points of Jewish theology, did they still argue politics? Did Sophie tell him how she sneaked into the darkened alcoves at shul to eavesdrop on Hebrew lessons, how she slopped across six miles of swale and dale to devour the precious volumes of Dostoievski and Tolstoi that slept in the dusty regional library? Did she tell Shia that when a political dissident hid out in Shumilina and began teaching night classes, she became his star pupil, sopping knowledge the way her older brothers sopped gravy with rye bread? Sophie was the first girl in Shumilina to attend high school—they didn't even have a women's bathroom then, she used the toilet at a neighboring family's house—but when the dissident encouraged her to pursue higher education in Vitebsk, Sophie's pious mother (*God sat in her hands*) forbade it, said Jewish girls must not learn unkosher things, need only learn what leads to successful village life. Were these the topics that Shia and Sophie discussed across eight epistolary years? At a certain point we must admit that they were love letters. When Sophie's parents understood the nature of these letters they banned them, so Shia and Sophie wrote to each other through another relative, sub rosa.

One day Shia rode into Prairie Grove, visited the general store, then the post office. A letter was waiting for him. He read it once and shoved it into his satchel.

That night he reread the letter while the firelight from the potbellied stove played across the earthen roof. Were his hands shaking? Can we assume otherwise?

Sophie was coming. No one could stop her.

5.

Forgive me—I'm moving well ahead in time now, for this is Sophie's story just as much as Shia's.

Sophie is an old woman, a grandmother, and her sweet grandson Howard—beloved boychik and mazik extraordinaire—is sitting at her knee in Winnipeg's old North End absorbing her fantastical stories. She is chain-smoking, ashing down the front of an old housecoat decorated with food stains and patterns of tiny rosebuds. Her enormous breasts sleep in her lap like toy dogs and her eyes are magnified behind grubby eyeglasses. Sophie is mischievous and doting, exuberant but cored with iron—for she has lived through all manner of privation and loss across these decades. Just as Shia grew burly on the plains of Manitoba, so too has Sophie. "I'm five feet tall and five feet wide," she tells little Howard, patting her stomach, "built to pull the plow, not walk behind it." *Harvard* she calls him, winking, Yiddishizing his name, playing games with her accent, which is still pronounced after nearly forty years in Canada. She rubs her grandson's Johnny Unitas buzzcut. He is in the second grade.

On Bannerman Avenue, where the tailors and metal scrappers and cabbies all live, Sophie has been telling little Harvard how she and Shia fell in love across nearly a decade of letters that found their way from Shumilina to the Canadian prairie, a story she will tell and retell as he grows up, morphing details here, juicing lines of dialogue there—for how important, truly, are the *facts?* She is a yarn-spinner, our Sophie, inveterate and unrepentant.

Yes, of course her parents were horrified when they understood she intended to join Shia in Manitoba. Although it was Sophie's father who was most enraged. Her pious mother (*God sat in her hands*) was fond of Shia, but neither parent could grapple with the nature of the cousins' bond. It was true that Jewish law permitted marriage between first cousins, technically it could be done, but these were first cousins from identical twin sisters, and they'd grown up together, all those meals they'd shared, the sheer intimacy of it, they were nearly—

"I'm going," Sophie told them.

In secret she had been training her sister to assume the store's daily operation, and over the last five years had hoarded her money while she politely endured the stumbling flirtations of young men from the village who bought snacks and tchotchkes and overstayed their welcome. She had saved one thousand rubles, had bought herself a muskrat fur coat, a gold watch studded with tiny diamonds, a gold bracelet and chain, and a ticket for safe passage across the seas, one level above steerage, she wouldn't even have to travel with the teeming unwashed. The matter was settled.

Sophie's parents had never ventured more than ten miles afield and now their darling maideleh was headed over the edge of the earth. Before she left, Sophie convinced them to pose for a family photo, a dour tableau in black and white that she would later hang inside the sod house. This was the last time she saw them.

(ETYMOLOGY OF UNCERTAIN RELEVANCE TO THE STORY)

The Latin root at the heart of the word incest—*castus*—means "morally pure, guiltless, chaste." An even older root is buried inside *castus*, related to the verb "to cut." A man who is *castus*, then, has cut barbarism from his life, shorn himself of impurities. A *casta* woman is devout and reverent before God. The *in-* prefix negates this and leads us to incest, a word steeped to its bones in impurity, moral defect, and guilt.

6.

When Sophie stepped off the train in Prairie Grove weeks later, scanning the platform for that pale and underfed waif, that cerebral

student of the Torah, she was grabbed up by a broad-shouldered golem
with a thicket of red beard. Over the years Shia had grown dense
and muscled, ironbound, stout as a barrel of rainwater and equally
immovable.

Directly the cousins set out for the homestead in a two-wheeled
carriage drawn by a cow. "Even in Shumilina we have horses to draw
the cart," she told Shia with dawning—what? Was it terror? Dismay?
And here little Howard interjected (well, not *here* of course, but many
decades later): "Boba, it was an ox. Cows don't pull carriages." Boba
Sophie brushed ash from the front of her housecoat. "You think I don't
know this, Harvard? We had to milk it halfway through the journey."

In the morning she was taken aback by her new lodgings. "A cave,
Harvard! Can you believe it? When you walk in, the dirt rains down
on your head!" But Sophie had not come this far to be put off by
dirty fingernails. She'd never done manual labor before—her realm
being arithmetic, accounting, Sophie the family pet—but she labored
now. She learned to cook and bake and accommodate the noisy rabble
of seasonal harvesting crews, learned to stack grain and carry water,
learned how the hands ache and swell after hours of udder-pulling,
how the shoulders and forearms burn splitting log after log after log.
After a few months the new couple rode twenty miles into Winnipeg
to be married by Rabbi Kahanovitch, who never learned the nature of
their relationship. They had a baby born in that sod house and a baby
die in that sod house one month later, the cold slicing across the plain
and reaping all the weakest things, children and animals and pioneer
spirits cut down without mercy.

Sometimes in the late afternoon, while Shia ferried a load of milk
into town and the hired workers had gone home, Sophie sat alone in
the house and navigated nauseating swells of loneliness. She became
aware of how still the land was, how supremely empty. At dusk the
telephone lines edging their fields buzzed like cicadas, the cables rising
and falling in wavelets toward the horizon. Sophie wondered then at

the happy pandemonium that was Shumilina, those chaotic meals awash in lighthearted squabbling, her sister Rosa's rough familiar hands plaiting her hair. There were so many bodies in that house, so few beds, that Sophie often slept atop the enormous brick oven—*fifty loaves at a time it could bake, Harvard!*—clambered up and spun a nest of blankets on the warm brick, burrowed into its womby embrace while her siblings pushed together chairs and commandeered couches for the night. As the desolate Manitoban light fell around her she must have thought about the baby, about those ten uncanny months in which she had been two.

Sophie told Shia there would be no more babies until they lived in a proper house. "How, Boba?" little Howard asked and Boba Sophie dragged on her cigarette and crossed her legs decisively. "The house came quickly."

Eventually they sold their acres and bought a bankrupt hardware store in Spy Hill, Saskatchewan, discovered a mutual knack for business. They prospered, they multiplied. Then a faulty boiler set their store ablaze in the night and they fled, hustling terrified children into icy December air while fire crept apathetically throughout the building. They left, they began again. In Manitoba they invested in a general store and once again they prospered, albeit slowly, over a decade, the money coming grudgingly and in angry spurts, the way a tap sputters to life after the thaw. Finally they moved to Winnipeg, cosmopolitan hub, and by now they were fully assimilated, for Shia had decided there would be no more Yiddish, no more Russian, only English spoken. He practiced constantly, asked customers to critique his pronunciation, and by the time little Howard came to know his grandfather (he was JB now, Shia burned away in that fire) he was a nattily dressed businessman, a hay and feed purveyor, sporting Hathaway shirts and cashmere coats and fluid English. He had come a long way from the farmboy rabbinical student in disintegrating shoes. And whenever little Howard asked his grandfather about the old days, JB wouldn't discuss it. "That's the past, Howard, I'm not interested in the past. Let's talk about today."

The fire burned clean their last physical connections to the old world—all the love letters burned and the gold jewelry burned and the muskrat coat burned and the books in Russian burned and the family photographs burned, along with all the letters Sophie had exchanged with her family after arriving in Canada (for she wrote them faithfully from the sod house, and they were relieved, although still unsettled). All the intricate threads that knitted them to the past turned to ember. Shia and Sophie were firmly of the new world now.

Let's call this the end of their story. Sophie raised four children, monitored their schooling and religious instruction. She joined ladies' clubs and beat women at mahjong, fostered a vibrant community for her family in Jewish Winnipeg. And when her children grew up and gave birth Sophie spoiled and delighted the grandchildren, as is right and proper, like little Harvard who sat at his grandmother's knee. And even little Harvard grew up and had children of his own. One of his daughters was named Ellen.

Reader, I married her: and Sophie and Shia's forbidden blood sings in her veins, and it sings in the veins of our children.

(FAMOUS PEOPLE WHO BY VARIOUS DEFINITIONS
WERE INCESTUOUSLY MARRIED)

Albert Einstein
Charles Darwin
The Outlaw Jesse James
Charlotte Perkins Gilman
Saddam Hussein
Abraham Maslow
Gautama the Buddha

Edgar Allan Poe

Igor Stravinsky

Mario Vargas Llosa

H.G. Wells

The Reverend Ilsley Boone (founder,

American Association for Nude Recreation)

Wernher von Braun

Sergei Rachmaninoff

Queen Victoria

Zeus

7.

In her many ravelings and unravelings of the family yarn, Sophie impressed upon Howard that her marriage to Shia would have been prohibited had they stayed in Shumilina. Their relationship violated no specific commandment, religious or legal, although it clearly discomfited those dearest to them. When they came to Canada they never disclosed the nature of their bond.

Their union today would be illegal in many of the United States, even criminal in some of them, although not in Canada, nor in much of the wider world. First cousin marriage is legal throughout South America, the Middle East, Australia, Europe, most of Africa, and some parts of Asia. It is here that Americans often raise the issue of birth defects, straining for some genetic and scientific objectivity: culturally acceptable, yes, but first cousin marriage is wrong because it harms the children, no? It is true that the risk of chromosomal abnormality rises just over 1% for the offspring of first cousins. Yet if this were actually an insupportable figure, then we would also ban American women in their early forties from giving birth, which bears a nearly identical increase in chromosomal abnormality. But we don't, and of course we shouldn't—these notions all dwell in the realm of eugenics, that well-trodden terrain of Nazis and dystopian sci-fi bureaucrats.

Our most intimate bonds (of family, of relatedness, of romantic love) operate on strange hidden frequencies. They defy easy categorization and pat analysis. We tell ourselves the rules of this domain are natural and immemorial—but they are always constructed and often very recent. We build temples to enshrine these rules, and sometimes their structures are sound and sometimes their gilt façades mask places where the beams of logic have long rotted away.

Perhaps all I'm saying is this: each of us must examine the narratives that have been presented, knock their walls for soundness, and choose whether to accept or reject.

(EMAIL FROM MIKE)

Sophie did not have big tits.

8.

I said before that we had reached the end of Shia and Sophie's story, but this is not entirely true. No stories have ends, just waypoints and pauses and junctions where the steel tracks slide onto another trajectory.

In the early 1940s, the lines of communication with Sophie's family in Shumilina fell silent, and she became worried. Her parents, her siblings, her other cousins—she couldn't reach any of them. By 1943, the rumors in Canada were rife, and by 1944 there were photographs. A great fire had burned through the land.

By 1950, when little Harvard was in the second grade, he would come to Boba Sophie's house after school each day (it was next door to his own) and slurp barley soup while she dictated letters in Yiddish. He would copy the words into English, his chubby fingers gripped earnestly around a pencil, tongue tucked between his teeth in concentration, carefully placing his letters on lined notebook paper. The Red Cross had established displaced persons camps throughout Europe, nodes of communication where family members might reunite, and Sophie and little Harvard sent letter after letter to these camps. "We are looking for the family named Nechamkin from the village of Shumilina near Vitebsk in Belarus," they would say. "If you know anything about the fate of these people, please write to us."

It was in this way and over some years that Sophie learned what she already understood to be true—that everyone she'd ever known there had been murdered. With Operation Barbarossa underway, the mobile killing units of the Nazi Einsatzgruppen moved across the countryside, village to village, commanding families to dig ditches and then executing them by rifle at close range. Mothers lay shielding terrified children and the soldiers shot the mothers and rolled the corpses off and then shot the children. Brothers watched their siblings slain in a heap and waited for the lights to be cut. Everyone Sophie loved in the old world fell into those pits: her parents, her sisters and brothers, her cousins and second cousins and friends and teachers. The village of Shumilina didn't exist anymore. The fire burned everything.

(A PARENTHESIS)

(But even this is not entirely accurate, for many years later Sophie discovered a single family member had survived. After Sophie left for Canada, her sister Rosa went to work as an apprentice at a factory making munitions for the Russian Army. In this role Rosa developed a specialized skill as a machinist. With the approach of the Germans imminent, the Russian Army packed up entire factories and shuttled them by train across the Urals, along with any workers in possession of unique skill sets. So it went with sister Rosa, who lived out the war in a small industrial town far into the Russian interior, where nearly a decade later Sophie reached her by letter—the first in a chain of correspondence that would last until Rosa's death from old age.

It is in moments like these that the arbitrariness of fate is so starkly on display. Due to simple love-drunk bullheadedness, Sophie was spared the hasty graves where her parents and siblings were slaughtered; Rosa dodged her execution because she could operate a machine. Both of their realities shifted a few degrees off the axis of the possible, steel tracks bearing Sophie to the port in Saint Petersburg, bearing Rosa across the Urals, bearing so many others to enormous ovens and ditches and empty tiled rooms.)

9.

Howard is telling me about the cleansing of Shumilina on tape, and as I play it back I can hear his voice thickening with emotion. Here again all the voices are overlaid—Sophie is telling little Harvard the story and Howard is telling me the story and behind that I can hear Ellen making breakfast for our kids, who are hollering and calling for more pancakes. Later we'll head to dinner at Uncle Mike's house, where he and Howard will argue about who has the details right, bickering and laughing as brothers must, but right now Sam is parping on a kazoo, trying to distract our interview, and Eve is squirming onto my lap to hear Grandpa Howard's story, and Mara has thrown her bowl of strawberries onto the floor, yawping barbarously at her newfound fine motor skill.

Sometimes when the day begins, when I dress Mara at the changing table, when I kiss the sacred rolls of her toddler armpits and pull mismatched socks over the tender pebbles of her toes, I think about how none of this would be without Sophie's forbidden love for her cousin. Howard and Mike would not be, and Ellen would not be, and Sam and Eve and Mara would not be. Sophie barreled off for the horizon against all plea and censure, lived in defiance of what was expected of her. Shia too rejected the offered path, refused the system intent on grinding his body to meat. He chose life in all its filth and hungers. This pair lurks in the corners and crannies of my days, my secret patrons and protectors. Onto what trajectory would my life have shifted had they chosen otherwise twelve decades past? And what choices have I similarly made, or shrunk from, and who will harvest their fruits in some distant year?

So sometimes in the morning's holy hush, when everyone else is still bundled under blankets, I think about Sophie and Shia—how theirs is the most beautiful incest story I know. I try to imagine the character of the light as it broke over the Manitoban prairie in those early hours, the potbellied stove now lit, thin huffs of brewing coffee on the air, as they cracked their door to the day. Shia is thinking about that afternoon's milk delivery and Sophie is fiddling with her husband's shirtsleeve, the two of them looking across the land, picking out the invisible markers and hidden signposts that will guide their passage through this new world.

HALLUCINATION (HOTEL ROOM)

I WAS LOOKING OVER THE FLAT MUDDY SPAN of the Ohio River from a hotel room in Cincinnati, several stories up, when I saw a woman down at street level. She was likely in her early twenties, the picture of carefree bohemian funkiness: her hair was up in two spritely knobs and she was wearing rainbow-striped tights and combat boots. This was early on a gray Saturday morning, and the woman was the first sign of human industry I'd seen. From my vantage I could watch her coming up the block beneath me, skipping really, and maybe humming, a tumbleweed of bright motion. Then I saw the woman whirl back laughing and aim a comment at whoever was coming up the sidewalk behind her, wagging her finger in a kind of lighthearted mock-remonstration. From my angle I couldn't see the rest of the sidewalk, so I couldn't see the person she was addressing. Something about this woman, something in her coltishness, in her electrified felicity—it reminded me of my daughter Eve, who had arrived now somehow in the fourth grade. The pixie woman bopped along, illuminating the puddled sidewalk as she went, occasionally laughing and calling back over her shoulder to the unseen interlocutor. It was a thrilling sensation, as if I'd been given a glimpse into my own child's future.

Just beyond the edges of my vision it seemed the hotel room had begun to stretch and warp in subtle fashion. I pressed myself flush against the window to get a better angle; in a moment I'd be able to see whom she was talking to. I realized I had become perhaps irrationally invested in this moment, excited for whatever happy adventures awaited her, and Eve too, and perhaps even registering mild twinges of paternal concern. The other person was hanging back. I assumed it was a man, although I didn't have specific evidence to support this. Then the woman froze and spun around, suddenly furious, her body rigid, her eyes wild. She began pointing and shouting at the person. From my height of several stories, and through the thick hotel windows, I couldn't physically hear what she was yelling—but the movements of her mouth, of her body, were immediately familiar: *Fuck you. I will fucking kill you.* She was jabbing her finger in repeated needle punctures aimed chest-level. The hotel room had taken on a deep chill—the air conditioner was thrumming and rattling in its metal casing and I snapped it off, straining to glean even a fragment of meaning from the exchange below. And then, just as suddenly, the woman laughed defiantly and with great full-bodied enthusiasm presented the mysterious pedestrian with her middle finger, then pivoted and continued skipping up the block.

She was laughing again, singing, and occasionally she would stop and turn and wave, then do a little pirouette, and sometimes she would nod agreeably, as if the person had made an excellent point. By now I could see that no one was behind her. The woman started yelling across the street, where there was certainly no one. She was throwing up her hands in frustration, shaking her head, then laughing again, doubled over in hilarity, skipping, flushed with an impossible joy, she was running now, sprinting, and then I couldn't see her anymore.

GARDEN OF THE GOATHERD

Just outside the Minneapolis city center, Hidden Beach is secluded along the wooded shoreline of Cedar Lake. The beach is cordoned off from the public eye by decommissioned train tracks and parkland and a tangle of leafy residential streets. A summer day there will see dreamy hula hoopers, families lounging on blankets, fire dancers, Rastas, and ideally the Mud Man—all coexisting beneath wandering lonely clouds of Purple Kush.

One afternoon I explored the woods at Hidden Beach with a man named Jesse, who works for a forestry service called Diversity Landworks. Jesse wanted to introduce me to his contract workers, who were currently undertaking an experimental program to rid the parkland of buckthorn, an invasive shrub that erodes the soil along the forest floor.

We found his team in a newly cleared elm thicket, drawn by their plangent bleating: fifty-six Kiko goats, thigh-high and butter-colored, bent to the work of extirpation.

Hidden Beach is frequented by members of the traveler and gutter punk scene, youthful wanderers and intentional transients, inked and pierced and lugging their possessions in teetering overstuffed packs. In a certain light Jesse might have been mistaken for one of their tribe: he had blonde dreadlocks tucked under a cap, formerly gauged earlobes, and a lip disc. In prior years he had hopped freight trains, slept in the open air, but he was happy now working as an urban goatherd, a job that complemented his contemplative nature. As we toured the buckthorn removal site, a summer snowstorm of white cottonwood fluff drifted through the elms. Two young goats were grappling and playfighting nearby. The rest of the herd nibbled leaves and stripped bark, masticating in peculiar side-to-side motion, and throughout the glade buckthorn demolition continued apace.

Jesse was proud of his charges. Just four days into the project, they were already well ahead of schedule. As we surveyed the site, he explained how the goats worked in concert to attack the buckthorn. One or two of the older females would climb onto a tree and bend it over, allowing the younger animals to strip leaves they couldn't reach on their own. This specific team was comprised almost entirely of females and kids, with just a few wethers—castrated males—in the herd. Intact males were counterproductive to a project like this, known as "prescribed browsing." The uncastrated males were intensely odoriferous (the result of pheromones and their habit of dousing themselves in their own urine), as well as sex-hungry to the point of distracting the females from their work. If there was a broader comment to be made about gender dynamics, Jesse chose not to make it.

Diversity Landworks is part of a burgeoning cohort of agribusinesses that use goats to solve specific land management problems. In the South, their target is invasive kudzu; in the West, goats are often used to create firebreaks; and along the Eastern Seaboard, teams of caprine commandos were dispatched post–Hurricane Sandy to eat through organic debris. In Minneapolis, where the parkland is too dense for a prescribed burn and often too steep to haul in stump grinding equipment, Jesse and his goat patrol present an elegant and herbicide-free solution to an aggressive invader like buckthorn. The goats find even the most abrasive plants alluring, having evolved in arid environments where spiky flora is the norm.

A few nights later I returned to visit Jesse, who was living in the woods with the herd throughout their contract at Hidden Beach. It was approaching midnight when I texted him from the edge of the elm thicket. A moment later, I followed the glow of his phone as it bobbed through the bosky darkness like a bioluminescent insect. He emerged from the gloom trailed by several Kiko goats, who took in my presence through their uncanny rectangular pupils, heads cocked. Then they wandered off to a late buckthorn snack.

We made our way across a tangle of roots and fallen deadwood to Jesse's camp, where he had strung a hammock between trees. A tarp shielded the hammock from rain and a multicolored knot of solar-powered Christmas lights hung beneath the tarp, a mellow deep-woods reading lamp. He told me it was strange to be in the woods in a city. Jesse could sense the people all around him, in the neighborhoods, just out of reach, yet he was alone here.

As we sat beside a low smoldering campfire, Jesse talked me through his routine. During the day he checked the fences to make sure there were no breaches, did occasional headcounts, attended to the goats' water supply and general wellbeing. He had become, to his own surprise, an easygoing ambassador for the goat patrol, which drew inquisitive beachgoers to the fence. "Normally I'm super shy," he said, "but here it's been *Blah, blah, blah, goats, goats, goats*. It's been really fun to talk to people."

Once darkness fell and the goats settled in for the evening, Jesse would cook himself a small meal, often with foraged ingredients— his dinner that night featured nettles paired with spikenard tea—and then strum his guitar or read. At night the main concern was security. Hidden Beach had been nude-friendly back in the 1980s, and it retained a shaggy bohemian vigor into the present day: at dusk, stoned fire dancers often whirled amidst a network of double- and triple-decker hammocks strung between the trees. A similar goat browsing treatment had been attempted in the neighboring city of Saint Paul, but one of the goats had been abducted in the night (and later safely recovered following a police chase). Jesse intended to see that no such hircine hijackings would occur on his watch. During his week at Hidden Beach, a handful of intruders hopped the double fence, but most people he caught were apologetic and vaguely embarrassed, some were drunk, and everyone left peacefully, disarmed by his amiable demeanor.

The night I visited, no one tried to sneak in. Our conversation was scored by the chirping of frogs and the soft lapping of Cedar Lake. Eventually it was time for me to go. Jesse escorted me to the tree line, along with a cadre of goats who trundled and snapped through the darkness. The animals watched me impassively at the fence, then returned to the woods to sleep.

On a warm October day, I left Minneapolis and drove several hours into the Driftless Area, in the far southeastern corner of the state. The Driftless is a geologic zone that covers parts of Iowa, Wisconsin, Illinois, and Minnesota, a region the glaciers of the last ice age never touched, never scoured flat into prairie. The zone is riverine, cut with valleys and studded with bluffs, Appalachian in appearance—rolling forested land bearing the secrets of subterranean caves and underground waterways.

In Houston, Minnesota (population: 1,033), I met Jesse at a coffee shop. It had been several years since I'd seen him last. We headed farther into the Driftless along new blacktop that curled around the bases of bluffs. Nothing was perpendicular, the county road uncoiling and acquiescing to the contours of the land. We passed farms where big barns were coming into their picturesque desuetude, red paint faded coral, boards rotting, a landscape filled with architectural memento mori.

Down an unmarked path we parked and scrambled up into the bluffs, aiming toward a goat browsing site. Diversity Landworks had been running a multiweek job, contracted by the state DNR, ridding the terrain of buckthorn and other invasives to help the rattlesnake population recover. When Jesse told me this, I glanced at my flimsy running shoes, my bare lower legs. "I guess I should have mentioned that earlier," he said, his tone somewhere between bashfulness and amusement.

Jesse is in his later thirties, his dusted blue eyes the color of an Oxford cloth schoolboy shirt. He has a firm handshake and scarred muscular forearms, both arising from years of physical labor. As we hiked he lugged a forty-pound car battery up into the hills to charge the portable electric fencing, which ran on solar power as well. His blond hair was up in a knot under a weathered baseball cap. He wore two days of scruff on his face and dirt under his fingernails.

In the intervening years, I'd forgotten Jesse's funny sly intelligence, his genial self-deprecation. When I apologized for running late, he responded with equanimity. "If Tardiness were a deity," he texted, "I'd be its high priest." As we climbed higher into the bluffs he began to call amiably to his charges, and soon clusters of goats began to materialize from the trees, nosing eagerly into the feed bucket he carried. Some reared up with their hooves on his back and he playfully shoved them off. As the goats snacked, he sketched their histories for me—which one had been healed of a broken leg, which pair had lost their mother young and been bottle-fed by him. "These two dweebs are really friendly," he said, gesturing at the mottled pair, then allowed himself a moment of what sounded like paternal pride. "They're super adorable."

We climbed higher into mustard-colored sandstone and rested in a scooped-out cave. A contingent of goats had accompanied us. The cave walls were pocked and undulating, worn by eons of wind and rain. At the top of the bluff, we sat looking out over soybean fields. Everything we could see had once been underwater.

Jesse grew up in a farm town in central Wisconsin, maybe a thousand people. His mother had him when she was eighteen and his father drifted

in and out of his life in complicated fashion. "I was a weirdo there," Jesse
said of his hometown. He knew he was bound elsewhere. "I realized I
could stay and be a farmer, or work at the feed mill, or the cheese factory,
or I could get the fuck out and do something"—the planet's oldest song.
He had gone to college for a bit, was highly literate and curious, but the
academy as an institution held slim appeal.

In his twenties, Jesse had stayed for a while in La Crosse, Wisconsin,
tucked along the banks of the Mississippi. One day he wandered down
to the riverfront and there encountered The Miss Rockaway Armada,
a punk collective that had built a fantastical barge from scavenged
junk material. The group was in the process of navigating down the
Mighty Mississipp', had made it 150 miles already. They had docked in
La Crosse to have a parade, mingle with the local vagabond counter-
culturati, maybe couch surf for a night. Jesse got to talking with the
river punks and went home buzzing. "I thought, shit, if these goofballs
can float down the river, then I can do all the things I want to do."
Their whimsical project had opened vistas in his imagination. "It was
an example of another world, in the world we live in."

So Jesse split La Crosse and began hitchhiking around the country
with friends, later train-hopping. With his partner at the time, he rode
the boxcars out to California and the Pacific Northwest, hopped trains
out to Maine and bindlestiffed up and down the East Coast. One
night in Maine they were given shelter by a slick-talking dude who
was caretaking a house out in the sticks. As they partied, the host's
girlfriend came by, then another buddy, and it took a few mentions of
how they were all going to "have some fun" before Jesse and his partner
understood they would need to politely bow out of that evening's
intended activity of group sex. (This was after the host had shown off
his knife collection.) Another night they slept in a boat in a boatshed,
awoke to find themselves hitched and hauled toward water before they
jumped out, grabbing clothes and shoes and waving apologetically to
the puzzled teen at the wheel of the truck.

One winter Jesse took a break from traveling and returned to La Crosse. In the spring he asked around for places in need of laborers and was pointed toward the Wiscoy Valley in Minnesota, where a back-to-the-land commune had set up shop in the 1970s. He pulled buckthorn all spring and by summer had wandered farther down the road to the property of a man who lived on six hundred acres. Carl was an old plant wizard, Jesse said, a charismatic curmudgeon hungry for acolytes, and maybe for company. He let Jesse live on his property, taught him all about the native flora, how to gather seeds responsibly, which plants had what curative properties and for what ailments. Some days Carl paid Jesse to do physical labor on the land, other days he paid him to "re-tune the waterfall," which involved moving rocks around in the river to change the frequency of the burbling.

Other likeminded folk began to migrate that way, for if you could be useful on Carl's acres, you were welcome. It was there Jesse met Kyle and Tim, who would become his close friends. In contrast to the intentional community down the road, Jesse felt they had formed an "unintentional community," a haven for kooks and wanderers, people who wanted to be good environmental stewards and who weren't terribly keen on engaging with the broader machinations of late capitalism. Jesse and his buddies worked and learned and lived on Carl's property in harmony, right up until they didn't, since all utopian societies end.

Before it was time for them to shove off, though, Carl called the three friends together. *I've got one word for you fellas*—(Did he really say it like that? Am I mythologizing ol' Carl, whom I've never met?)—*and that word is goats.*

Goats? they said.

Goats, Carl said.

Jesse and his buddies went off into the world, agreed that Carl was right. They would buy some goats to work the land, and before long they had twenty goats, and then sixty goats, and they had something called Diversity Landworks, something called a business. Kyle and Tim would be co-owners, had secured the funding, and Jesse—he of agrarian background, who had run away from farm life way back when—would provide the cultural and historical knowhow to make things operate smoothly (like how to appease a farmer, for instance, when, hypothetically speaking, their goats damaged a man's cornfield). Each year the business grew. In the summers they often scored browsing contracts on Minneapolis parkland, and Jesse would go where the job took him. Only in the urban areas did the goats require an overnight chaperone, but out in the Driftless, where they based their operations, there was always choring to look after, labor to be done.

Up on the bluff, Jesse and I sat in the warm October breeze, taking in the view. He had a lot of time to think when he was with the goats. He'd been contemplating what it meant to be an invasive species in a place, and how we define those terms—what things we call weeds when they're actually native, what invasives we decide have value because they look pretty. He'd spent hours and hours rambling through these bluffs, studying the flora; he pointed toward a distant cliff where he believed indigenous people had camped long before, said the vegetation up there was out of place, cultivated.

Sure, he got lonely sometimes, but he was happier out in the natural world. And he could always pass the time reading or playing music. I thought then of the shepherds I'd known in Lesotho, boys who drifted across the mountainside by themselves, strumming homemade instruments and singing to their flock, weeks and months spent in deep isolation. Then, as Jesse was showing me a picture on his phone, a notification popped onto the screen. It was filled with heart emoji; someone had just matched with him on Tinder.

A moment of silence elapsed.

"Pay no mind to that," he said drily, the tiniest hint of a smile on his lips.

Out across the valley the first golds and oranges were starting to pop amidst the green. In a few weeks goat season would be finished. Soon Jesse and Kyle and Tim would dismantle the various browsing sites, pack the goats into trailers, transport them back to the farm. They would hunker down for winter.

FAREWELL TRANSMISSION

AFTER DARK THE GHOSTS COME.

First the homebound sun must complete its golden transit, drawing down through the mountains, the cloudbanks blooming orange then violet. Shepherds guide their cattle toward the kraal and to bed, and this whole time of day clatters with the rhythm of hoofbeats. It is called mantsiboea, this hour, when the falling light wakes up the wine-red veins of the earth. Children return to the hearth now and soon they will burrow into warm beds while their grandmothers whisper them full of ghost stories.

Only much later, at the bottom of the night, only then do the ghosts come: shades flitting between boulders and creeping from clefts in the earth. They have been listening to the stories the grandmothers tell (for even spooks enjoy hearing their pranks exaggerated to rapt audiences), and so they spur themselves to bolder feats of paranormal mischief. They have waited for their allotted time and now saunter brazenly through the villages, scampering across thatched roofs, rattling windowpanes, and tipping portions of piled-stone walls. They are not meanspirited, per se, just hungry for attention.

One night I sat out late with Bokang talking about ghosts and stars. This was in Lesotho, riven with gorges, cloudskirted at elevation, where the basalt teeth of the Maloti Mountains jag through the country and down into South Africa. My wife and I had been coming here from the U.S. since 2007—her work is in anthropology, mine is in pretend journalism—and on recent stays our two small children joined us.

I found Bokang at the guard shack stoking a small fire, his balaclava pulled down and his eyes shining in the dark. It was June, full winter, that dry time of year when the acrid scent of burning is always on the wind. I had known Bokang for nearly a decade by this point, a thin and sinewy man a few years older than me, whose primary affect I came to think of as sleepy joyfulness. He worked as the night watchman at a rural safe home where orphans and vulnerable children were temporarily housed, a place where my wife and I had lived and worked over the years. Bokang's transition to guard duty had come later in his career: he was nearly forty now, but spent most of his early years laboring as a herd boy in the craggy alpine highlands of Mokhotlong district, coaxing meandering sheep through mountain passes and grappling with donkeys—those odd endearing beasts whose stubbornness is softened by their liquid eyes, portals to a world-weary intelligence. Shepherding requires either a hard-driving nature or a gentle and patient one, and Bokang's was of the latter variety.

I poured us some whiskey into a battered tin cup and set out my tape recorder. I was gathering information about the night sky and knew Bokang could speak knowledgably on the topic of Sesotho stars, which differ from American stars or Chinese stars or Finnish stars, the heavens having a cultural dimension in addition to the scientific. As he pulled up his balaclava, his breath joined mine. Bokang was staring down long icy nights in the guard shack. The fire popped and rustled beside us as we talked, sending shadows skittering along the ground.

"That one is Tosa," Bokang said, sipping from the cup and pointing to what I later learned was Jupiter. Then he gestured to Venus, currently playing the role of the evening star. "And that one is Sefalabohoho, which in Sesotho we can call those crusty scrapings at the bottom of the pot. If you are traveling to a village when you see Sefalabohoho, then that is the food remaining for you—meaning it is a star for latecomers." He told me how the seven stars of Selemela instruct when the planting season should begin in the spring, then swept an arc overhead, tracing the broad bright smear of the Milky Way. "And that we can call Molala, the neck."

Bokang learned these astronomical elements as a small boy on the mountainside with his flock. The older shepherds coughed as they drew on hand-rolled spliffs, buds of crumbled dakha laced amidst the tobacco, and explained to Bokang that Molala was the spine of the universe. Around the campfire they shared the secret histories of stars with him, although sometimes they told hushed tales of what witches could do while you slept. Bokang wasn't yet ten. Later, his parents took him out of the mountains and sent him to primary school. For several years he balanced his studies with shepherding work, even went to secondary school for a few years—a rarity for herd boys—but by the time he turned twenty, both of his parents had died. Bokang became head of household then, left school, took on other work to provide for his five younger siblings and the two cousins who lived with them. Later he secured this job on the night watch, which paid well. He was now "the leader," he told me, responsible for siblings and cousins, his own wife and children, various nieces and nephews.

Through the windows of the safe home, I could see one of the house mothers pacing in the darkened nursery, singing to a child she held in her arms. Bokang and I briefly discussed a trip out to Manamaneng, his village, several hours through the mountains, where I had long promised to visit. Then I sipped from the whiskey cup, breathing caramel and campfire smoke, and asked Bokang if he wanted to hear a ghost story. It involved Motsi, I told him, the other night guard, a frail older man whose voice sounded of cobwebs and the dusty corners of unused cupboards. Bokang nodded, began to chuckle quietly in anticipation.

"This is all true," I said. "Or at least this is what Motsi told me."

Motsi had been cataloguing types of Sesotho ghosts at my request, describing things like obe, for instance, the creature that sneaks into locked houses to kidnap people. Once inside, obe will tuck an unlucky sleeper into its giant flapping ears and whisk him off. You may wake one morning, Motsi told me, utterly disoriented and lost on some distant plateau, only to realize you have been captured by obe in the night. Then there is thokolosi, a gnome-like figure that sends people into paralyzing trances while they sleep, or even sepokho, a kind of ghost that will rise from its grave to torment people. If you find yourself visited by sepokho at night, you must go to a traditional healer, ngaka ea Sesotho, someone who can prescribe the appropriate medicines to ward off these unwelcome spirits.

Other ghosts are less malicious, Motsi told me. Sometimes the dead do not receive a good funeral and so they visit their living relatives to complain. These ancestors speak to people through dreams, sometimes send a toothache as a message, all to communicate their displeasure—they are too hungry, the grave is too cold. The best solution is to make amends: you must slaughter an animal and prepare a feast, with a tiny portion of everything set aside for the unhappy spirit: a sip of tangy homebrewed joala, a bite of mutton, a torn hunk of steambread, still dense and doughy. Then present the food and tell the ghost its meal is ready, prepare the skin of the slaughtered animal and say its blanket has been found. Once satisfied, the restless soul can return to its grave.

Motsi had been talking me through this spectral taxonomy one night, his voice croaking and guttering in the dark, when he fell silent. The old man's voice was hushed when he spoke again, his eyes candled with a strange urgency. A few nights back, he said, he caught someone on the property. He was walking the grounds, slowly, slowly, as I had seen him do many times before, rattling the chains on the gates, testing the door to the storage shed—but when he came to the garden he stopped. There at the far end, in the middle of the cabbage plot, stood an old woman. She stared at Motsi, mute, rhythmically sweeping gentle arcs with a broom made of long grass. Motsi knew immediately this woman was a witch, had likely been traveling through the air on spider webs, when one snapped and dropped her there in the garden. The monkey that would have been riding on her back must have scampered into the bushes—Motsi thought he could hear it rustling down by the river. The two stood watching each other.

Then the woman spoke. She told him she had been inside the safe home, had visited the children's room.

Motsi considered the matter carefully. On the hillside he could hear the devil dogs slipping through the underbrush, scrapping and whining as they met in darkness. Motsi knew he was protected by powerful medicine and by his ancestors as well—that these were likely the forces that had snapped the witch's web as she passed overhead. He knew she couldn't hurt him, but he was unsure about the children splayed out asleep in the nursery. Several more times the witch called out to Motsi, whispering unspeakable things, trying to goad a response from him. But Motsi had the advantage: if you can remain silent, he told me, the witch is bound to the spot; the moment you speak, the trap is broken and the witch will dart back into the sky.

And so Motsi remained silent throughout the night, standing vigil as she lurked in the far corner of the garden. The night took on a deep chill and the stars rotated through the firmament. The witch swept her broom incessantly, staring at Motsi with baleful eyes.

At daybreak, when the morning star Mphatlalatsane winked over the mountains, a man arrived at the property. He claimed to be the son of this old woman, said she had wandered off in the night and he had been searching for her. Motsi looked at her then with fresh eyes: in the daylight, she seemed disoriented and feeble, uncertain where she was. Motsi decided to let the man enter. The son then took the old woman by the arm and escorted her tenderly from the grounds. As they passed, the son thanked Motsi for watching over his mother, and the old woman hissed that she would discover his heavy medicines, she would be ready for him next time.

By the time I finished relaying the story of Motsi and the witch, Bokang and I had emptied a good portion of the whiskey cup. We sat on a low wall outside the guard shack, our heels kicking time against the smooth cement.

Bokang had a broad smile on his face.

"No," he said, "Motsi did not tell me about that encounter."

"Well," I asked, "what do you think? What do you know about those creatures—sepokho or obe or thokolosi?"

Bokang began laughing, a soft percolation that warmed our roost. "The thokolosi?" he said after a moment. "I can't see it. You can hear people talk about it, but you can never see it."

Bokang hopped down from the ledge and prodded the edges of the fire. "We Basotho people, because we are very brave, we need to make a person afraid of something. So this is why they named something thokolosi—to scare children, to make them afraid so they will listen to you. You can also hear women talking about koko, that the children should behave or koko will come for them. But you can never see it."

"So you don't believe these things exist?"

Bokang looked off to the side for a moment, then back at me.

"Maybe some people will argue that they exist, but I can't see them."

"But do you think they exist and you just haven't seen them yet— or you think they don't exist at all?"

Bokang gave me a sly smile and was silent for a moment. I hope he understood my needling was only in the spirit of campfire conversation, when certain matters can be discussed openly under cover of darkness. When I listen back to the recording now, I am struck by the way he framed his answer. Bokang was an empiricist, but he was careful not to value his own truth more highly than another person's.

"I have more than thirty-nine years," he said. "Maybe next year I can have forty. But I haven't seen any of those things."

Then he paused, grinning, and knocked back the end of the whiskey. "Maybe they can sense that my blood is very strong."

That was all a few years ago.

We sat out late that night, Bokang and I, talking about stars and ghosts. Bokang is a ghost now too, one who lives in my headphones. The recording I made is his last physical trace—(*as long as we live, he too lives, and is become a part of us*)—and as such it is a sacred artifact. I had no way of knowing it was the last time I'd see Bokang, that, as the Sesotho idiom goes, he would become needed.

Certain memories of him are prominent: the time he guided me proudly through town on horseback, the both of us wrapped in heavy wool blankets decorated with maize cob pictograms. He led me that day to some informal shebeen, and in the cramped dark of the room we joined old men passing around a coffee can filled with sour homebrewed joala. We sat in the gloom of that place, our clothes steeped in sweat and cookfire smoke, while someone played traditional Sesotho songs on a battered cassette deck that had persisted well into the digital age.

I remember too his goofy gentleness with my children—Bokang would direct Sam and Eve in morning calisthenics before the dew burned dry. Horses stood asleep in misty fields while he exhorted the five-year-old and three-year-old toward crispness of form in their jumping jacks, cheered their studious attempts at lunges, then demonstrated his proficiency with a homemade barbell: coffee cans he'd filled with cement, planted at the ends of a metal bar scavenged from the roadside.

Frequently I found Bokang along the dusty road through town, standing beside a blue tarp arrayed with the day's produce: pyramids of dented apples, banana bunches, leafy basketballs of cabbage. He and his wife loved to kibitz with passersby, forever giving away more fruit than they sold.

These memories are all scored by the sound of his laughter, which Bokang conducted with an orchestral nimbleness—leading with a spritely piccolo that resolved into cello thrum and popping percussives. Although the precise character of his laughter always depended on the specifics of the off-color joke you had just told him.

Other memories are lost forever. Or at least they hide away, waiting for their allotted time, when they can creep from mental clefts and flit from behind psychic boulders and visit me at the bottom of the night.

On New Year's Day—when the summer in Lesotho is bright and pulsing, the air aglide with scanning hawks, when the intersections clot with joyous drunk laborers home for the holidays—Bokang was stabbed to death by his younger brother, another man I knew well, a smiley joker who used to give my children money when he saw them on the main road.

Bokang had organized a feast that day in honor of his daughter, who had taken some award in grade seven. Relatives came, people ate and drank too much, and late into the party the two brothers argued over some family matter long stewing.

I wonder now, years later, how the younger brother must have stared down at his hand, the knife clenched and shaking in his grip, blood steadily pooling. Did he think then of those years when Bokang raised him? Is that too simplistic? Or was his mind only static: slow rolling waves of electric white.

But when I slip on my headphones and play the tape, Bokang waits somewhere just behind me, out of sight, the soft gauze of his laughter falling across the back of my head. As I write this, I'm the same age that Bokang will always be. I've had thirty-nine years now, and perhaps next year I'll have forty.

That final night, Bokang told me shepherds have many stories about individual stars, but no constellations exactly. I don't know if this is true, or if it was just true for Bokang, but it is a noteworthy cosmological perspective. After all, constellations are just stories we tell ourselves, attempts to impose order onto something beyond order. And ghost stories are the same, a rickety narrative framework we build around the ultimate lacuna, shaky wooden handrails beside the abyss. And the stars themselves are a kind of ghost story. Those points of light are vast thermonuclear explosions that happened long ago—blooms of cosmic violence in the wake of things that no longer exist.

So I rewind the tape and play it again. On the recording, Bokang is worrying about his sister, a police officer. There have been recent small-scale clashes between the army and the police and Bokang thinks his sister should leave the country—these are uncertain times. I fast-forward, now hear myself telling Bokang that we'll visit his village the next time we come to Lesotho. He has been speaking quietly, matching the mood of the late hour, but his voice rises when I say this.

"You will visit us in Manamaneng? *Hele*—we'll have a celebration!" A gentle laugh begins rising deep in Bokang's chest, expanding now, warm and pleasant and enveloping us like dough.

"Yes," he says, talking quickly, "I would like Sam to visit me there. He can play and follow after the other kids—"

Bokang breaks off, envisioning the scene, our children playing together by his hearth, his laugh still bubbling through my headphones. And I think somehow we will do this, it must be possible still. There is a field where the mountains sit down against the earth, the valley carpeted with dense purple scrub, and tiny coins of snow hide there in the vegetation. Sam and I will ride out beneath the morning star and find Bokang with his animals, gathering sheep for the celebration. We will lead the animals home to be slaughtered, and while the meat is prepared we will sip joala, pass it around the circle, and the smoke from the cookfire will wash over and purify us.

CODA

HALLUCINATION (SAN SEBASTIAN)

From the esplanade we watched a woman walk the dark and empty sea. She was curved like a questionmark, navigating shinhigh swells with hand crutches, bowed in monkish concentration. The sand sucked at her crutchtips. The woman's hair was white and chopped, gnarled in the wind. We leaned against a wrought-iron railing, looking over the water as if from balcony seating, and from our vantage the beach curled like a scimitar around the bay. The woman's right leg shone an angry pink against the marbled gray water: it was heavy with edema, a painful swollen tube she urged along. Her seawalk had the air of daily repetition, some salt-brined therapy, weather be damned—it was misting now, the result of a storm that had paced the horizon for hours, throatclearing and sweeping clean the beach before arriving as this: suspended vapors, nothing more.

For a moment I wondered if the woman was hoping to be raptured in the sea—but no, I had it all wrong, rapture is a kind of flight from difficulty and this was altogether different. The seawalker was in vigorous disputation with the physical world—crutchtip, crutchtip, steady, absorb the wave's impact, balance against the wind, drive the swollen leg forward—a dogged rebuttal to her own tenuousness.

We left the Spanish seaside and began our ascent. Myself and my wife, her brother, his wife. We switchbacked up the mountain through sheets of vegetation that spilled down to the water. The four of us scampered along the road, euphoric and alert, the land pulsing with viridescence. This is when I understood the LSD had begun to bite. My body's screws were tightening with pleasing simultaneity, squeezing excess air from the gaps between organs, everything cinching, bringing the physical self to a state of density shot through with mild lightning. I was myself, only more so.

We came to a bend in the road that looked across the bay. Far below, the seawalker trudged on, a tiny pink gem chip, the grand expanse of gray velvet. I was steeped in giddy goodwill. Beneath my feet the road was vibrating just so, nearly below the perceptual threshold, and a thought skittered through my mind about the astounding tenuousness of, well, everything. I ran for a bit. The mist blew off and left a coastal chill.

Soon we reached the mountaintop where a small amusement park was perched: a charming rundown hamlet composed of log flumes and rusting trampolines and haunted houses made to look like Swiss chalets. It was more surprising than anything I could have summoned with my mind. The amusement park appeared to be a relic of the 1960s, never renovated, its premier attraction a rollercoaster that on crumbling concrete track hung its riders out over the sea. We strapped in and in my American watchfulness I understood the ride had never heard the lilting tune of regulatory engineering code, its tracks untouched by gloved inspectors' caress, and through my joyful buzzy grinning I knew that I would die. The amusement park with its mountainous shoulders only shrugged, dragged upon its celestial Gauloises, said *Yes, it's true, we all must die.*

We lived. And when the rollercoaster docked we sprinted toward the bumper cars with a mania perhaps accessible only to the recently pardoned. There we began a merry game of attempted homicide—the four of us, adults by legal definition—T-boning and whiplashing each other, saucer-eyed and cackling. Ellen cracked me from behind hard enough to make my molars ache.

In that caged square, where the air was suffused with diesel sweetness and singed rubber, cascading with electrode sparks, only one other car was in motion. It was piloted by a father and son, the boy four or maybe five, sweet and simmering with nervous joy. One side of his face drooped around the eye, some congenital accident of birth, and he was scooched back into the warmth of his father, whose arms were around him and on the steering wheel. They zipped and darted, crashing into empty bumper cars. I thought of my own small children, none of whom were very small, and all of whom were far away.

And then for a moment I came to that holy place where the ego dissolves slightly—where the self steps away from centerstage and fades back toward the wings, peers from curtain's edge out toward the crowd. You can see the faces of the audience from that angle, bathed in unguarded wonder, can see the actors from a new vantage, whiskers showing through their greasepaint. How long had I been girding myself against different kinds of endings, against the rending of bodies and cleaving of families, against the flattening of fragile things? The relentless question of *after*. Suddenly it was in my head how there would come a time when I was gone and I would never know the lives my children were living, how they would have successes and devastations that would never reach me, there would be no me to reach. One day I would never again see Sam's goofy smirk as he made a dirty pun or the fastidious way Eve aligned her cheese slices on lunch bread, would not look upon Mara's vibrating glee as she explained the rules to a game she'd played in gym class. They were each a singular intelligence, as was Ellen, as was I, as were my parents, my siblings, everyone I knew, each one a matchless efflorescence of energy and motion, never to be repeated.

Yet what I felt was not sadness but a strange and disorienting gratitude. What improbable bounty, that we might share these unpromised years, that we might be temporary together. In the same flashing instant I could see how our days were consequential due precisely to their fleetingness. That endlessness leached meaning. Death was not the opposite of life but its prerequisite.

Later, after we had come down from the mountain, and after I had left Spain entirely, I would remember that epiphanies are always a kind of banality, that their tenuous magic takes effort to sustain beyond the dreamstate. I would attempt to sit gracefully with this thought—that temporariness is what gives our lives significance—but I was only imperfectly successful. If I was intentional I could dwell in the sensation of gratitude again, but that anticipatory ache over the endings of things would seep into the room like mist, and I knew this was equally true. They made uneasy traveling companions. They would have to coexist.

And later still, I would learn there are ways of transcending even the necessary finitude of death—for what is a boundary if not something to disregard?—when I read the words of a theologian named Karen Teel. She had been ruminating on her mother's death and had come to see the loss in this way: "My mother's love for me did not begin or end with her. She could love me because others loved her, they could love her because they had been loved. Her love is with me now. And it will continue, through me, through everyone I love, through everyone they love, long after we are all forgotten."

And even later, at a point not yet arrived, I will learn other ways to confront the vital fact of death, and then other ways still, and all my attempts and methods will contradict each other and complement each other and drift me further from certainty, since certainty in this realm is the only guarantee of hollowness.

But all of that comes later—let's linger for a moment at the mountaintop in the bumper cars, where my body is charged through and humming, where the ego has not yet shouldered its way back to centerstage to resume its monologue. Somewhere far below is the seawalker, wincing as she plants each crutchtip, plodding forward. Up here I've been watching the father and son, observing the boy with the drooped eye. He is snugged into his father's arms, surveying the chaos that surrounds them, wary of the four derelicts orbiting his field. We are vectors of anarchy and disarray. Now I see him come to some decision, he whispers to his father in words I will never hear.

There, he points, singling us out, *and there*.

The boy's father grins sharkishly and begins to hunt us for sport. We slow down and are overtaken, one by one, we howl as each of us is smashed, we flail our arms in buffoonish defeat. The boy with the drooped eye claps and claps and shakes his father by the arm.

Again, again, he points,
all our fragile bodies ricocheting
                             &
        around around the sparking
                      world
           spins

NOTES

Bird & Spade

The William Stafford poem I mention is "Traveling through the Dark."

The Kings of Simcoe County

A version of this essay first appeared in The Morning News.

Huron River Drive

A version of this essay first appeared in Black Warrior Review.

A Noose in Hentiesbaai

A version of this essay first appeared in Guernica.

While researching historical, cultural, and geographic elements of this essay, I relied on the following works:

Bley, Helmut. *South-West Africa under German Rule*, 1894-1914. Northwestern University Press, 1971.

Bridgman, Jon. *The Revolt of the Hereros*. University of California Press, 1981.

Carroll, Faye. *South West Africa & the United Nations*. University Press of Kentucky, 2014.

Drechsler, Horst. *Let Us Die Fighting: Namibia under the Germans*. Lawrence Hill & Co., 1981.

Ellis, Justin. "Report on the Registration and Election Campaign in Namibia, 1978". Christian Centre of Namibia, 1978.

Gerwarth, R. and Malinowski, S. "Hannah Arendt's Ghosts: Reflections on the Disputable Path from Windhoek to Auschwitz". Central European History 42.2 (2009): 279-300.

Green, R., Kiljunen, M.L., and Kiljunen, M., eds. *Namibia: The Last Colony*. Prentice Hall Press, 1981.

Olusoga, D. and Erichsen, C. T*he Kaiser's Holocaust. Germany's Forgotten Genocide and the Colonial Roots of Nazism*. Faber & Faber, 2011.

Rotberg, Robert, ed. Namibia: Political and Economic Prospects. Lexington Books, 1983.

Keyhole to Sana'a

A version of this essay first appeared in The Atlantic. If you want more of the delightful Ali Sultan, go check out his comedy album Happy to Be Here, where you can hear me guffawing loudly in the background. Also worthwhile is the podcast he hosts with his mother, Mona, called Stories with My Muslim Mom.

Death of the Virgin

A version of this essay first appeared in The Southeast Review. In writing about Caravaggio's life and works, I relied on two fine books: Andrew Graham-Dixon's Caravaggio: A Life Sacred and Profane (W.W. Norton & Company, 2012) and Helen Langdon's Caravaggio: A Life (Farrar, Straus and Giroux, 1999).

Peanut's Odyssey

While the writing, reporting, and interviewing in Cliff's story is all original work, I relied on Stephanie Clifford's excellent journalism in The New Yorker to help clarify technical aspects of the judicial and criminal justice systems.

Ballad of the Curtain Jerker

There are many people more knowledgeable about professional wrestling than me, among them Oliver Lee Bateman and David Shoemaker, whose writing provided essential historical and cultural context about the squared circle. Either one of them could tell you what a curtain jerker is.

The Open Pits

A much shorter version of this essay first appeared in Pacific Standard (RIP). The Joan Didion line is from her book Slouching Towards Bethlehem. And I could not have completed this piece without the help of Tselane Mokhethi, an excellent friend who occasionally worked for me as a translator. She helped conduct interviews in English and Sesotho and did invaluable work translating and transcribing the results of those conversations.

Steel Tracks

Much of the general content and dialogue in this piece comes from oral history conveyed by Howard & Mike Block, fine burly men whom I am certainly not afraid of, and whom I could defeat in an arm-wrestling contest or other feat of strength, if so challenged. But all the granular detail, all the color and specificity, anything that makes this story hum—it comes from Sophie's personal correspondence.

Garden of the Goatherd

The beginning half of this essay first appeared in Pacific Standard, where the editor Ryan Jacobs, in his benevolence and wisdom, allowed all my dumb goat wordplay to stand untouched.

Farewell Transmission

Tselane Mokhethi again provided essential interpretation, translation, and transcription work. Fezekile Futhwa's book Setho: Afrikan Thought and Belief System was an excellent resource that illuminated aspects of Sesotho cosmology and astronomy. The title of this essay (and of the book as a whole) is a nod to Jason Molina and his song "Farewell Transmission" (recorded under the alias Songs: Ohia). That song, and the troubled nature of his life, provided thematic inspiration throughout the course of this book.

Hallucination (San Sebastian)

Two outstanding books were rattling around my brain when I wrote this essay: Lincoln in the Bardo, by George Saunders, and The Fire Next Time, by James Baldwin.

CREDITS

MANY PEOPLE MADE THIS.

Bestowers of the priceless gifts—time, stories, advice, insight, support, and encouragement:
Maura Costello, Ali Sultan, Ryan Becker, Kristen Santillo, Devon Monroe, Arik Cannon, John Maddening, Howard & Mike Block, Jesse the Goatherd, Ntate Motsi, Tselane Mokhethi, Andrew Rose, Dan Sheehan, Jennie Rothenberg Gritz, Nick Jackson, Ryan Jacobs, Jennifer Sahn, Steph Opitz, Jason Diamond, Joni Tevis, Eli Saslow, John Brandon, Wells Tower.

Several patient souls read earlier versions of these essays and improved them free of charge. Send me an invoice:
Tristan Harter, Rosangel Cruz, Jessie Foley, Angela Pelster, Katrina Vandenberg, Inara Verzemnieks, Curtis Sittenfeld, John Brandon (second time in the credits, showoff).

Although no one has given me more thoughtful feedback over the years than one of the finest writers I know:
Dylan Walsh.

A book on the shelf is placed by many hands:

Michelle Dotter and the dedicated people at Dzanc Books.
Rachel Vogel.

That outrageously good cover! Those sneaky illustrations! Thank you:
J. Zachary Keenan.

One of the reasons to keep fighting:
Cliff Jones.

Not gone, never forgotten:
Willie, Bokang.

Rogues, scoundrels, and assorted bad influences:
Mary, Dylan, John, Claire, Anne, Ryan, Emily, Chris, Dan, Maura, Howard, Julia, Sheila, Jim, Gussie, Nthabeleng, Neo, and the Bo-Lephoto crew.

My first and most enduring teachers:
Bill McGrath & Mary Quinlan-McGrath.

<waving hand in front of face> "Stinky!":
Sam, Eve, Mara

She who defies superlative and qualifier:
Ellen Block.

ABOUT THE AUTHOR

Will McGrath has worked as a reporter, homeless shelter caseworker, public radio producer, UPS truck loader, Burger King chicken sandwich mayo-applicator, ghostwriter, and ghosteditor, in slightly different order.

His debut book, *Everything Lost Is Found Again*, won the Society of Midland Authors Award for Biography & Memoir, as well as the Dzanc / Disquiet Open Borders Book Prize.